Birth control

DATE DUE

MAR 18 2014			

Demco, Inc. 38-293

Birth Control

Other Books of Related Interest:

Opposing Viewpoints Series

AIDS

Childbirth

Reproductive Technology

At Issue Series

Sexually Transmitted Diseases

Current Controversies Series

The Abortion Controversy

"Congress shall make
no law . . . abridging
the freedom of speech,
or of the press."

First Amendment to the U.S. Constitution

The basic foundation of our democracy is the First Amendment guarantee of freedom of expression. The Opposing Viewpoints Series is dedicated to the concept of this basic freedom and the idea that it is more important to practice it than to enshrine it.

OPPOSING
VIEWPOINTS®
SERIES

Birth Control

Beth Rosenthal, Book Editor

GREENHAVEN PRESS
A part of Gale, Cengage Learning

GALE
CENGAGE Learning™

Detroit • New York • San Francisco • New Haven, Conn • Waterville, Maine • London

12|08

Christine Nasso, *Publisher*
Elizabeth Des Chenes, *Managing Editor*

© 2009 Greenhaven Press, a part of Gale, Cengage Learning.

Gale and Greenhaven Press are registered trademarks used herein under license.

For more information, contact:
Greenhaven Press
27500 Drake Rd.
Farmington Hills, MI 48331-3535
Or you can visit our Internet site at gale.cengage.com

For product information and technology assistance, contact us at

Gale Customer Support, 1-800-877-4253
For permission to use material from this text or product, submit all requests online at www.cengage.com/permissions

Further permissions questions can be emailed to permissionrequest@cengage.com

Articles in Greenhaven Press anthologies are often edited for length to meet page requirements. In addition, original titles of these works are changed to clearly present the main thesis and to explicitly indicate the author's opinion. Every effort is made to ensure that Greenhaven Press accurately reflects the original intent of the authors. Every effort has been made to trace the owners of copyrighted material.

Cover photograph reproduced by permission of Adam Gault/Digital Vision/Getty Images.

LIBRARY OF CONGRESS CATALOGING-IN-PUBLICATION DATA

Birth control / Beth Rosenthal.
    p. cm. -- (Opposing viewpoints)
    Includes bibliographical references and index.
    ISBN-13: 978-0-7377-4194-0 (hardcover)
    ISBN-13: 978-0-7377-4195-7 (pbk.)
    1. Birth control--Moral and ethical aspects. I. Rosenthal, Beth, 1964-
    HQ766.15.B57 2009
    363.9'6--dc22
                                             2008026069

Printed in the United States of America
1 2 3 4 5 6 7 12 11 10 09 08

Contents

Chapter 3: Should Teens Have Access to Birth Control?

Chapter 4: What Should Teens Be Taught About Birth Control?

Why Consider Opposing Viewpoints?

> *"The only way in which a human being can make some approach to knowing the whole of a subject is by hearing what can be said about it by persons of every variety of opinion and studying all modes in which it can be looked at by every character of mind. No wise man ever acquired his wisdom in any mode but this."*
>
> *John Stuart Mill*

In our media-intensive culture it is not difficult to find differing opinions. Thousands of newspapers and magazines and dozens of radio and television talk shows resound with differing points of view. The difficulty lies in deciding which opinion to agree with and which "experts" seem the most credible. The more inundated we become with differing opinions and claims, the more essential it is to hone critical reading and thinking skills to evaluate these ideas. Opposing Viewpoints books address this problem directly by presenting stimulating debates that can be used to enhance and teach these skills. The varied opinions contained in each book examine many different aspects of a single issue. While examining these conveniently edited opposing views, readers can develop critical thinking skills such as the ability to compare and contrast authors' credibility, facts, argumentation styles, use of persuasive techniques, and other stylistic tools. In short, the Opposing Viewpoints Series is an ideal way to attain the higher-level thinking and reading skills so essential in a culture of diverse and contradictory opinions.

In addition to providing a tool for critical thinking, Opposing Viewpoints books challenge readers to question their own strongly held opinions and assumptions. Most people form their opinions on the basis of upbringing, peer pressure, and personal, cultural, or professional bias. By reading carefully balanced opposing views, readers must directly confront new ideas as well as the opinions of those with whom they disagree. This is not to simplistically argue that everyone who reads opposing views will—or should—change his or her opinion. Instead, the series enhances readers' understanding of their own views by encouraging confrontation with opposing ideas. Careful examination of others' views can lead to the readers' understanding of the logical inconsistencies in their own opinions, perspective on why they hold an opinion, and the consideration of the possibility that their opinion requires further evaluation.

Evaluating Other Opinions

To ensure that this type of examination occurs, Opposing Viewpoints books present all types of opinions. Prominent spokespeople on different sides of each issue as well as well-known professionals from many disciplines challenge the reader. An additional goal of the series is to provide a forum for other, less known, or even unpopular viewpoints. The opinion of an ordinary person who has had to make the decision to cut off life support from a terminally ill relative, for example, may be just as valuable and provide just as much insight as a medical ethicist's professional opinion. The editors have two additional purposes in including these less known views. One, the editors encourage readers to respect others' opinions—even when not enhanced by professional credibility. It is only by reading or listening to and objectively evaluating others' ideas that one can determine whether they are worthy of consideration. Two, the inclusion of such viewpoints encourages the important critical thinking skill of objectively evaluating an author's credentials and bias. This evaluation will illuminate an author's reasons for taking a particular stance on an issue and will aid in readers' evaluation of the author's ideas.

It is our hope that these books will give readers a deeper understanding of the issues debated and an appreciation of the complexity of even seemingly simple issues when good and honest people disagree. This awareness is particularly important in a democratic society such as ours in which people enter into public debate to determine the common good. Those with whom one disagrees should not be regarded as enemies but rather as people whose views deserve careful examination and may shed light on one's own.

Thomas Jefferson once said that "difference of opinion leads to inquiry, and inquiry to truth." Jefferson, a broadly educated man, argued that "if a nation expects to be ignorant and free . . . it expects what never was and never will be." As individuals and as a nation, it is imperative that we consider the opinions of others and examine them with skill and discernment. The Opposing Viewpoints Series is intended to help readers achieve this goal.

David L. Bender and Bruno Leone,
Founders

Introduction

> *"In cultures where women bear and breastfeed children throughout their reproductive years, it's normal to have few menstrual periods."*
>
> *—Harvard Women's Health Watch*

> *"The hype surrounding these new ways of taking hormonal contraceptives is focusing negative ideas about women by making normal menstruation into a problem; and the health implications of these more continuous ways of administering higher doses of estrogen and progestin are not yet known."*
>
> *—Jerilynn C. Prior*
> *and Christine L. Hitchcock,*
> *The Centre for Menstrual and*
> *Ovulation Research*

The U.S. Food and Drug Administration (FDA) approved the birth control pill in 1960. Since then, a variety of contraceptives have become available that allow women to regulate their menstrual periods. Depo-Provera, which is injected every three months, was approved by the FDA in 1992. Seasonale, approved in 2003, reduces monthly periods to once every three months. In July 2007, the FDA allowed Lybrel to be sold to the public. Taken every day, this birth control pill stops a woman's menstrual cycle—it prevents her monthly period, which is called "menstrual suppression."

This has presented society with a new series of dilemmas about contraception. Advocates of menstrual suppression contend that it is not necessary for women to menstruate monthly if menstruation is painful to the point of incapacitation and if it interferes with a woman's daily activities. Opponents maintain that there are health risks to consider and that suppressing menstruation can affect a woman's feelings about herself and her place in society.

A woman taking a traditional oral contraceptive will take three weeks of pills that contain a combination of progesterone and estrogen, and menstruate during the one-week period when she takes placebo pills. The same hormones are used in Lybrel, albeit in a lower dose, but Lybrel is taken every day without any placebo pills.

Wyeth, the manufacturer of the new pill, says it is intended for women who suffer from endometriosis, as well as from the effects of a painful menstrual period, which can include heavy bleeding, headaches, mood swings, and cramping. "The symptoms that often accompany menstruation—from depression to bloating and headaches—can significantly disrupt women's lives," said Dr. Kurt Barnhart, an associate professor and director of clinical research for the Department of Obstetrics & Gynecology at the University of Pennsylvania School of Medicine and a consultant to Wyeth, when presenting the results of a survey about menstruation suppression at the Association of Reproductive Health Professonals' 2007 conference. "Menstruation is not medically necessary. Now that we have products that have proven to be safe and effective at suppressing menstruation, we can offer increasing options for women."

There also is the issue of convenience. The ability to avoid a menstrual period at an inconvenient time appeals to many women as well. An April 20, 2007, *New York Times* article reported that Dr. Ginger D. Constantine, therapeutic director for women's health for Wyeth, stated that research funded by the company found that "women often feel less effective at work and school during their periods. They limit sexual activity and exercise, wear dark clothes, and stay home more, resulting in absenteeism."

Some research has shown that the possibility of endometrial cancer and ovarian cancer may be lowered because of birth control pills. Lybrel is relatively new to the market so there is not yet research available about the effects of taking it for an extended period of time, but the known risks are comparable to those found in traditional oral contraceptives—the chance for strokes, heart attacks, and blood clots.

Opponents worry about the physical and mental effects of enabling women to stop their periods. As already discussed, there are questions about the long-term effects of the medication, particularly on adolescent girls. Doctors caution that women using Lybrel need to take pregnancy tests more often because they might not realize they're pregnant if the drug fails. Research has found that women taking the drug experienced spotting or light bleeding (breakthrough bleeding) even though they didn't have regular periods.

There are concerns about how helping women to eliminate their periods affects their feelings about being women, how they view themselves as part of society, and how society as a whole perceives women. "Young girls have their work cut out for them as it is in our culture; they shouldn't have to battle a barrage of negative and misleading messages about a natural bodily process on top of the other challenges they face," writes Kiescha McCurtis in the November/December 2007 issue of the *Women's Health Activist*. For McCurtis and others, menstrual suppression only reinforces the idea that something is wrong with menstruation—that it is somehow an unnatural process that should be hidden from society.

As the arguments surrounding this issue indicate, birth control involves many complicated issues. The ethical concerns about menstrual suppression mirror many of the other arguments over contraception. For some, teens should be taught about only abstinence because sex education will only encourage them to have sex, while others believe that it is unrealistic to think that kids will promise not to have sex.

These arguments are examined in chapters that ask the following questions: How does birth control affect society? Who should control access to birth control? Should teens have access to birth control? What should teeens be taught about Birth Control? The viewpoints presented in this volume examine how birth control continues to divide American society.

CHAPTER 1

How Does Birth Control Affect Society?

Chapter Preface

On September 28, 2000, the U.S. Food and Drug Administration (FDA) approved mifepristone, which is also known as RU-486, or the "abortion pill." This prescription-only drug ends an early pregnancy, which is classified as forty-nine days or less from the start of a woman's last menstrual period. RU-486 stops progesterone, which is a hormone that gets the lining of the uterus ready for a fertilized egg and helps sustain a pregnancy.

According to a January 22, 2008, *Washington Post* article by Rob Stein, "At a time when the overall number of abortions has been steadily declining, RU-486-induced abortions have been rising by 22 percent a year and now account for 14 percent of the total—and more than one in five early abortions performed by the ninth week of pregnancy." Danco Laboratories, which manufactures mifepristone, reports that 840,000 American women have used it.

Supporters of RU-486 maintain that it is a safe, nonsurgical alternative for women who need to end a pregnancy. They are critical of opponents who argue that the use of mifepristone has led to deaths and infections, and are concerned that their goal is to make abortion illegal again. According to NARAL (National Abortion Rights Action League), "In fact, the most serious threat to women's health is making abortion illegal: In 1962, about one million illegal abortions took place, and more than 5,000 women died as a result (the numbers may have been even higher due to inaccurate autopsies). That equals a fatality rate of at least one in 1,000, or 114 times that of mifepristone."

Abortion opponents reject mifepristone because they reject abortion, whether it is a surgical or a chemical procedure. They also contend that the drug was not tested properly before its approval and point to incidents of the deaths of several American women after the drug was taken to prove that it is dangerous. The National Right to Life Committee argues, "Virtually every chemical abortion comes with substantial pain and bleeding. Many are accompanied by gastrointestinal side effects such as nausea, diarrhea, and vomiting. To the callous these can be labeled inconveniences for some women, but these sometimes turn into risky complications for others. These symptoms, however, are nearly identical to signs of other more serious problems such as infection or ruptured ectopic pregnancy. With both patients and doctors expecting these as typical side effects of the chemical abortion process, they easily might fail to consider or check for other causes like infection or ectopic pregnancy until dangerously late."

Intertwined in the debate over birth control is the issue of abortion, which leads to a discussion of the right to privacy and what that entails. Supporters of birth control argue that men and women have the right to decide privately about using contraception. Opponents contend that the right to use contraception is not about privacy because it affects a human life, which they believe starts at conception. The authors in the following chapter debate the effects of birth control and emergency contraception on society.

"The government doesn't have the right to tell women what they do in private. That's up to the women themselves."

Birth Control Is a Privacy Issue

Unitarian Universalist Association of Congregations

In the following viewpoint, the Unitarian Universalist Association of Congregations (UUA) contends that using birth control is a private matter. In Griswold v. Connecticut, *the group argues that the Supreme Court overturned the law that made contraceptives illegal because it came down to the right to privacy. The UUA maintains that there are still many efforts today—particularly in state legislatures—to reduce access to it, even though birth control was legalized in 1965. The UUA is a religious group that combines the traditions of the Universalists and the Unitarians. The two groups merged into the UUA in 1961.*

As you read, consider the following questions:

1. According to the UUA, what percentage of counties in the United States do not have providers who will perform abortions?

2. What word is not specifically mentioned by the Bill of Rights, as cited in the viewpoint?

3. According to the authors, what does the "gag rule" prevent the staff in clinics funded by the federal government from telling patients?

There are two generations of women alive now who have no memory of what life was like before abortion and birth control were legal in the United States. It was a different world, a world where unwanted pregnancies were terminated in alleys, filthy apartments, or—if money wasn't an object—in Japan, Mexico, France, or another more "progressive" country. And birth control? While we think of Margaret Sanger, the Unitarian crusader for family planning who coined the phrase "birth control" in 1915 and founded Planned Parenthood so that others would have a choice, there were many parts of the United States where birth control was outlawed decades after Sanger's death and where the "rhythm method" of family planning was the only one legally available to women.

Access Is Still Limited

In the course of less than fifty years, reproductive choice has changed dramatically. New, highly effective methods of birth control are widely—although far from universally—available. Abortion is safer, but 86% of U.S. counties have no provider, and fewer and fewer medical schools are training doctors to perform them. And while the issue of choice in birth control seems assured in most parts of the United States, efforts to limit access to contraception and abortion are alive and well in the United States, largely through state legislatures. Certainly, the matter of abortion rights is once again under attack. If we look back to the mid- to late 1960s, we can see the role courageous Unitarian Universalists played in making it possible for future generations to have a choice.

In Connecticut prior to 1965, there was no legal access to birth control for women or couples. State law, based on a statute formalized in 1879, prohibited use of contraceptives. Though several attempts had been made to change the law, all had failed. Those who worked for the Planned Parenthood League of Connecticut (PPLC), under the direction of Estelle Griswold, affirmed the right of women to choose to use contraception and helped women obtain such assistance through "border runs" to legal birth control clinics in Rhode Island and New York.

In 1961, Griswold and PPLC Medical Director C. Lee Buxton, an eminent Yale obstetrician/gynecologist, opened a birth control clinic in New Haven, hoping to test the 1879 law. The police raided the clinic; the two were convicted and the case appealed. The ruling made its way through the legal system and ultimately to the U.S. Supreme Court, where arguments were heard in 1965 (*Griswold v. Connecticut*).

While the case was in the courts, the PPLC offices had been shut down, but the women running the organization had become more committed than ever to providing women access to family planning methods. Vera Weiner, a member of the Unitarian Society of New Haven, along with Dorothy Giles, Louise Fleck, Marjorie Ullman, and others, decided that the clinic had to continue to operate even though the New Haven police had officially closed it.

Weiner and the others set up operation in the basement of the Weiner household in a suburb of New Haven. They put cardboard over the windows and engaged a registered nurse to dispense the newly-available birth control pill, as well as packages of contraceptive jelly, diaphragms, and vaginal foams, to all those who requested it. They set up typewriters and tables and went through the local newspapers, writing letters to all women whose birth announcements appeared in print, offering them contraception. They swore their families to secrecy about the operation and carried on, even though publicly, the clinic had been closed down.

Birth Control Is a Matter of Privacy

Weiner said at the time, "The government doesn't have the right to tell women what they do in private. That's up to the women themselves." Indeed, *Griswold v. Connecticut* was about the right to privacy, not specifically about birth control. On that basis, the Supreme Court overturned Estelle Griswold's conviction and invalidated the Connecticut law. Although the Bill of Rights does not explicitly mention "privacy," the justices of the Court found, by a vote of 7-2, that privacy was protected through the different clauses of the Bill of Rights.

Since *Griswold*, the Supreme Court has cited the right to privacy in several rulings protecting access to sexual health care, most notably in *Roe v. Wade* (1973). The Court ruled that a woman's choice to an abortion was protected as a private decision between her and her doctor. For the most part, the Court made these later rulings on the basis of Justice John Harlan II's substantive due process rationale, rendered in the *Griswold* case.

Vera Weiner died in 2006, and the women of the Unitarian Society of New Haven who joined in working for PPLC have all passed on. But their work, which kept the birth control clinic open during the time *Griswold v. Connecticut* was in litigation, helped ensure that women in Connecticut had choices for family planning. Vera's daughter Deborah writes, "I've always been astonished at the dedication my mother and those other women demonstrated when that struggle was going on. The legal risks they took were significant but still they persisted in doing what they thought was not only right, but just."

Extending That Privacy to Include Abortion

At nearly the same time, in Minnesota, a group of Unitarians and activists gathered to discuss how to obtain legalization of abortion in the state. In 1966, the group, including Bob Mc-Coy, a member of the First Unitarian Society of Minneapolis, founded the Minnesota Council for the Legal Termination of Pregnancy (MCLTP). MCLTP initially backed a bill which would allow abortions if approved by a committee of doctors, but soon adopted the view that abortion was a personal decision, and worked to completely overturn the state's abortion ban.

During these early years, MCLTP was based in McCoy's house and entirely run by volunteers who developed the board of advisors, organized volunteer activities, and worked on the political scene. Dr. Margaret Horrobin, Bob McCoy's spouse, remembers, "People called Bob to see if he could help them get abortions. I remember he had a call from someone in Chicago who had had an illegal abortion, and she was standing in a phone booth, bleeding." He said, "I have to find somewhere for these people to go." And so the office was headquartered in our house. Over the years we saw several thousand women. Bob had a crew of women who educated themselves into being abortion counselors, and they talked to the people who came. Our neighbors were very tolerant. . .there were people parked up and down the street [each night], waiting for their turn to talk to someone. The total number of women referred to California, Canada, and other places where abortion was legal, was huge. . .Bob sent over 9,000 people for legal procedures during those years.

MCLTP campaigned for legal abortion by establishing relationships with state legislators, hiring a lobbyist, and building a solid grassroots organization. In 1972, MCLTP changed its name to the Minnesota Organization for the Repeal of Abortion Laws (MORAL), reflecting its stance on repealing legislation that limited reproductive choice, and operated the sister organization Abortion Counseling Service (ACS). Margaret Horrobin recalls, "Bob relished debate, and got a lot of nasty letters, but he never backed down from speaking to groups." He was a good speaker and a salesman, and his territory covered Minnesota, the Dakotas, and Iowa. He would

Allowing Women to Make Their Own Decisions

By enabling women to control their fertility, access to contraception broadens their ability to make other choices about their lives, including those related to education and employment.

Since 1965, the number of women in the U.S. labor force more than doubled, and women's income now constitutes a growing proportion of family income.

- In 1965, 26.2 million women participated in the U.S. labor force; by 2005, the number had risen to 69.3 million

- The labor force participation rate of married women nearly doubled between 1960 and 2005—from 31.9 to 61

- In a 1994 survey, more than half of employed women said they provided at least half of their household's income

- Among married women who worked full time in 1993, women contributed a median of 41 percent of the family's income

- By 2005, 25.5 percent of women in dual-income families earned more than their husbands

- Between 1960 and 2005, the percentage of women who had completed four or more years of college more than quadrupled—from 5.8 percent to 26.5 percent

Susanne Pichler and Deborah Golub, "Griswold v. Connecticut: The Impact of Legal Birth Control and the Challenges That Remain," June 2007. www.plannedparenthood.org.

combine his selling trips with speaking on this subject. He would speak at the Unitarian Churches and fellowships, almost anywhere there was an audience.

When *Roe v. Wade* was handed down in 1973, MORAL's mission had finally been achieved and the Abortion Counseling Service was no longer needed. But McCoy's dedication to helping women receive essential legal medical care to end unwanted pregnancy had become a lasting legacy that shaped the formation of NARAL [National Abortion Rights Action League] Minnesota. . . .

Using the Gag Rule to Prohibit Birth Control

In the 1970s, money for family planning became available under Title X of the Public Health Act and Title XX of the Social Security Act. Beginning in 1980, the Reagan administration, and later the Bush administration, worked to restrict Title X by imposing a gag rule on the staff of family planning clinics. Upheld in 1991 by the Supreme Court in *Rust v. Sullivan*, the gag rule prevented staff in federally funded clinics from telling patients about all options for managing a pregnancy, including abortion. PPLC and other family planning clinics around the U.S. resolved to not accept federal funds with those restrictions.

With the election of President Clinton in 1992, the gag rule was overturned administratively for the duration of his term. Upon assuming office in 2001, however, President George W. Bush reinstated the global version of the gag rule (imposed on recipients of U.S. foreign aid), and further restrictions and application of the gag rule on Title X have been imposed during the Bush administration.

> *"But the Supreme Court soon trans-*
> *formed the 'right to privacy' (the refer-*
> *ence to marriage quickly disappeared)*
> *into a powerful tool for making public*
> *policy."*

Birth Control Is a Public Health Issue

Robert P. George and David L. Tubbs

Robert P. George, a professor at Princeton University, and David L. Tubbs, an assistant professor at King's College in New York City, wrote this article for the National Review. *In the following viewpoint, George and Tubbs argue that the decision handed down by the Supreme Court in* Griswold v. Connecticut *improperly extended the right to privacy to include too many generalities. They maintain that the Court's judgment in* Griswold *incorrectly led to* Roe v. Wade, *which stated that the right to have an abortion is one of privacy.*

As you read, consider the following questions:

1. According to George and Tubbs, what did *Eisenstadt v. Baird* establish?

2. What does the Fourth Amendment protect?

3. What was the name of the judge whose 1987 nomination to the Supreme Court was rejected because of his opinion of *Griswold v. Connecticut*?

Forty years ago [1965], in *Griswold v. Connecticut*, the Supreme Court of the United States struck down state laws forbidding the sale, distribution, and use of contraceptives on the basis of a novel constitutional doctrine known as the "right to marital privacy."

At the time, the decision appeared to be harmless. After all, *Griswold* simply allowed married couples to decide whether to use contraceptives. But the Supreme Court soon transformed the "right to privacy" (the reference to marriage quickly disappeared) into a powerful tool for making public policy. In *Eisenstadt v. Baird* (1972), the Court changed a right of spouses—justified in *Griswold* precisely by reference to the importance of marriage—into a right of unmarried adults to buy and use contraceptives. Then, in a move that plunged the United States into a "culture war," the Court ruled in *Roe v. Wade* and *Doe v. Bolton* (1973) that this generalized "right to privacy" also encompassed a woman's virtually unrestricted right to have an abortion.

Taking the Right to Privacy Too Far

No one doubts that there are true privacy rights in the Constitution, especially in the Fourth Amendment, which protects against unreasonable searches and seizures and ensures that warrants issue only upon a showing of probable cause that a crime has been committed. (Indeed, these rights prevented any kind of aggressive enforcement of the laws struck down in *Griswold*.) But the justices in *Griswold* produced a non-text-based and generalized right. "Privacy" functioned as a euphemism for immunity from those public-morals laws deemed by the justices to reflect benighted moral views.

The privacy decisions that sprang from *Griswold* have been widely criticized, and in the last 20 years there have been two notable efforts to silence and stigmatize that criticism. The first occurred in 1987, when a coalition of liberal interest groups helped to scotch Judge Robert Bork's nomination to the Supreme Court, partly because of Bork's misgivings about this novel doctrine. The second occurred in 1992, when the Supreme Court decided *Planned Parenthood v. Casey*, which reaffirmed the "central holding" of *Roe v. Wade*.

Neither of these efforts succeeded. To this day, millions of Americans cannot accept *Roe v. Wade* as constitutionally legitimate. And thanks to recent developments, public suspicion of the Court's "privacy" doctrine is now greater than ever.

Two years ago [in 2003], in *Lawrence v. Texas*, the Supreme Court pushed the doctrine into new territory by overruling *Bowers v. Hardwick* (1986), a decision that had upheld a state's authority to prohibit homosexual sodomy. But in *Lawrence*, Justice Anthony Kennedy provocatively remarked that *Bowers* was wrong the day it was decided. Criticism of the ruling in *Lawrence* intensified a few months later when the supreme judicial court of Massachusetts promulgated a right to same-sex marriage in that state. In *Goodridge v. Department of Public Health* (2003), the court cited *Lawrence* to support this newly minted right. It evidently mattered little to these judges that the majority opinion in *Lawrence* expressly denied that the case involved the issue of marriage.

As the courts push the "privacy" doctrine further and further, public criticism keeps pace. *Griswold*, however, has received little attention. Even harsh critics of *Roe* and *Lawrence* are loath to say that *Griswold* was wrongly decided. Most of those who worry about the judicial abuse of the right to privacy do not want or expect the Supreme Court to revisit the case. Yet the cogency of any serious critique of "privacy" may depend on the willingness to reexamine the roots of the doctrine in *Griswold*.

It's Not About Privacy—It's About Abortion

Consider abortion. Conceding the correctness of *Griswold* gives a huge advantage to the defenders of *Roe* and *Casey*. They benefit because so many influential jurists and scholars say that the "inner logic" of the contraception cases must yield something like *Roe*. Outsiders may regard this argument with skepticism, but its purpose is clear: It tries to smooth the road from *Griswold* to *Eisenstadt* to *Roe*—and beyond.

But one point is rarely mentioned. Even though *Griswold* was less consequential than *Roe*, the two cases suffer from similar flaws. The many shortcomings of *Griswold* are less well known, because the case is enveloped in myths.

In American law schools, decisions such as *Roe*, *Casey*, and *Lawrence* are widely praised—not because of their legal merits (which are dubious), but because they comport with the ideology of "lifestyle liberalism" that enjoys hegemony there. Consequently, since 1973 most legal scholars have had no incentive to reassess *Griswold*. But if *Griswold* was wrongly decided, *Roe*—intellectually shaky on any account—loses even the meager jurisprudential support on which it rests.

The lack of scholarly engagement with *Griswold* partly explains the myths now surrounding it. Exposing those myths further undermines the arguments for a generalized right to privacy.

Connecticut Had the Right to Regulate

Myth #1: The Connecticut laws were "purposeless restraints," serving no social interest.

Supreme Court Justice David Souter is one of several jurists to make this assertion. The confusion arises from *Griswold*, whose majority opinion nowhere identifies a legislative purpose.

For anyone who cares to look, the purposes of the laws are apparent in the record of the case: Connecticut sought to promote marital fidelity and stable families by discouraging at-

Expanding on the Right to Privacy Too Much

From contraceptives to same-sex marriage is a distance that no one 40 years ago could have imagined the courts would travel. The thread connecting them is *Griswold's* judicially concocted "right to privacy"—amorphous, free-floating, and wonderfully handy for writing judges' personal opinions into constitutional law.

Jeff Jacoby, "Privacy by Decree," Townhall.com,
Nov. 10, 2005, www.townhall.com.

tempts to avoid the possible consequences of non-marital sexual relations through the use of contraceptives. Prominent judges in Connecticut recognized the legitimacy of these purposes, and the state's supreme court upheld the laws against several constitutional challenges from 1940 to 1964.

Did Connecticut's policy go too far in its efforts to promote marital fidelity? Many thought so. But roughly 30 states regulated contraceptives in the early 1960s, and the uniqueness of Connecticut's statutory scheme was long recognized as its constitutional prerogative.

The Court Imposed Its Own Views

Myth #2: The decision in *Griswold* rested on some overarching or time-honored constitutional principle.

Ostensibly, that principle was "privacy." But the *Griswold* doctrine would have been unrecognizable to the Supreme Court even a few years earlier. In *Gardner v. Massachusetts* (1938), for example, the Court dismissed a similar challenge, noting that the suit failed to present "a substantial federal question."

In the majority opinion in *Griswold*, Justice William O. Douglas referred—as comically metaphysical as it sounds—to "penumbras [right guaranteed by implication] formed by emanations" of specific constitutional guarantees as the source of the new right. He had nothing else to go on.

Other jurists have since argued that the right to marital privacy could be derived from cases before 1965 involving the rights of parents to direct the upbringing of their children. But the cases they cite have little in common with *Griswold*.

What, then, was the operative "principle" in *Griswold*? Nothing other than the Court's desire to place its imprimatur on "enlightened" views about human sexuality. This project continued beyond *Griswold* and culminated in *Lawrence*, where the Court essentially said that all adults in America have a right to engage in consenting, non-marital sexual relations. Consistently missing from the Court's discourse on privacy, however, has been any discussion of parental duties, public health, and the welfare of children.

No Right to Override State's Decision

Myth #3: No sensible jurist or commentator would say that the case was wrongly decided.

In fact, two widely respected and sensible jurists, Justices Hugo Black and Potter Stewart, dissented in *Griswold*. Black was a noted liberal and, like Stewart, recorded his opposition to Connecticut's policy as a political matter. Yet both jurists insisted that the policy was a valid exercise of the state's power to promote public health, safety, and morals.

To Justices Black and Stewart, the "right to privacy" cloaked a naked policy preference. Justices in the majority were, without constitutional warrant, substituting their own judgments for those of the elected representatives in Connecticut. This, according to jurists across the political spectrum, is precisely what had brought shame on the Court during the "Lochner era," from roughly 1890 to 1937, when in the name of an unwritten "liberty of contract" the justices invalidated state social-welfare and worker-protection laws. But the crucial distinction underscored by Black and Stewart between the desirability or justice of a policy and the state's constitutional authority to enact it, lost much of its currency as the right to privacy expanded.

Griswold Would Not Be Passed Today

Myth #4: The legislation invalidated in *Griswold* might be widely used again if the case was overturned.

This line was often repeated in 1987 when Robert Bork was nominated to the Supreme Court. Meant to frighten ordinary citizens who approve of contraceptive use, this scenario simply fails to acknowledge changes in public opinion since 1965. Laws like those struck down in *Griswold* clearly have little chance of passing today even in the most conservative states.

Contraception Doesn't Justify the *Griswold* Decision

Myth #5: The widespread use of contraceptive in the United States today provides a *post hoc* [after-the-fact] justification for *Griswold*.

When *Griswold* was decided, adults could buy and use contraceptives in almost every state (despite various regulations on their sale and distribution). Given the social ferment of the 1960s and 70s, the Connecticut policy would sooner or later have been modified. But the ubiquity of contraceptives in America today does not justify *Griswold*—any more than the widespread use of abortion justifies *Roe*.

It might seem fanciful to say that the idea of a generalized constitutional right to "privacy" could now be repudiated; many believe that it has become an integral part of American law. But no one should accept this conclusion. The struggle against usurpations by the Supreme Court committed under the pretext of giving effect to unwritten constitutional rights has a historical precedent. As noted, from roughly 1890 to 1937, the Supreme Court invalidated worker-protection and social-welfare legislation on the basis of an unenumerated right to "liberty of contract." After much criticism the Court relented, and in 1937, announced that it would defer to legislative judgment where policies did not run afoul of constitutional principles. They promised, in short, to halt the practice of reading into the Constitution their own personal judgments about social and economic policy and the morality of economic relations.

The Supreme Court will not revisit the question of state or federal laws banning contraceptives. Yet the Court can and should find an occasion to admit that the manipulation of constitutional law that began with *Griswold* has been a colossal mistake. Such an admission would hardly be radical or, as we have observed, unprecedented. The Court's confession of error in repudiating its *Griswold* jurisprudence, far from harming its reputation, would enhance its prestige. We have no doubt that the same good effect would redound to the Court if the justices were candidly to speak the truth: The idea of a generalized right to privacy floating in penumbras formed by emanations was a pure judicial invention—one designed to license the judicial usurpation of democratic legislative authority.

"The same high-resolution ultrasound that makes you queasy about aborting a 12-week fetus has made it safer to perform abortions at four or five weeks instead of waiting."

Birth Control Results in Fewer Abortions

William Saletan

William Saletan wrote this article for the Seattle Times. *He writes about science and technology for the online magazine* Slate. *In the following viewpoint, Saletan contends that medical technology has led to such improvements in contraception that fewer abortions are being performed. He argues that the need for fewer second-trimester abortions will help make* Roe v. Wade *obsolete in time.*

As you read, consider the following questions:

1. Through the end of which trimester does *Roe v. Wade* allow the right to have an abortion?
2. According to William Saletan, by 2002, what percentage of women between the ages of 18 and 24 have used "emergency contraception"?

3. According to the author, from 1982 to 2002, by what percentage did contraception use rise and by what percentage did the abortion rate drop?

For the first time in 14 years, legal abortion in the United States is in serious jeopardy.

In recent weeks, the shape of this assault has become clear. First, on the morning of Justice Samuel Alito Jr.'s debut, the Supreme Court announced that it would review the constitutionality of the Partial-Birth Abortion Ban Act, setting up what anti-abortion activists hope will be the beginning of the end of *Roe v. Wade*. The next day, South Dakota lawmakers passed a ban on virtually all abortions, and abortion-rights groups vowed to litigate it all the way to the high court, which would force the justices either to overturn or reaffirm *Roe*. A few days later, the court told the abortion-rights side it could no longer use racketeering laws to halt blockades and protests at abortion clinics.

The impending legal battles put us on the verge of repeating the past two decades of the abortion war: anti-abortion victory, abortion-rights backlash. At the end of the cycle 20 years from now, we'll be right back where we are today. Unless, that is, we find a way out.

And that means moving beyond *Roe*.

Fewer Abortions Make *Roe* Obsolete

Politically, legally and technologically, the 33-year-old court decision is increasingly obsolete as a framework for managing decisions about reproduction. But only the abortion-rights movement can lead the way beyond it. The anti-abortion groups can't launch the post-*Roe* era, because they are determined to abolish its guarantee of individual autonomy, and the public won't stand for that. It must be up to reproductive-rights supporters to give the public what it wants: abortion reduction within a framework of autonomy.

Three political asteroids are heading toward us that make the latest round of the abortion confrontation inevitable. The first is the so-called "partial birth" abortion ban. Second, is the South Dakota law. The third is the potential retirement of Justice John Paul Stevens. The order in which they hit will determine how close *Roe* comes to being overturned. But one way or another, they'll reignite the cycle of victory, backlash, and defeat.

Six years ago, in the middle of the 2000 presidential campaign, the court struck down a partial-birth ban from Nebraska because it was too vague and lacked an exception for pregnancies that threatened the woman's health. The case, *Stenberg v. Carhart*, was decided on a 5 to 4 vote. Anti-abortion groups faced a choice: Add a health exception to the federal partial-birth bill to get it through the court, or refuse and gamble that a future court, populated by justices chosen by President [George W.] Bush, would reverse *Stenberg* and uphold the ban.

They gambled, and the gamble paid off. In July 2005, a week before an appeals court sent the federal ban toward the Supreme Court, Justice Sandra Day O'Connor, the fifth vote in *Stenberg*, announced her retirement. Her replacement by Alito creates an almost certain five-vote majority against *Stenberg*. Justices don't overturn precedents casually, but *Stenberg* is far more vulnerable than *Roe*. *Roe* is more than three decades old, was a 7 to 2 decision, has been used as a basis for subsequent Supreme Court opinions and was reaffirmed under fire 14 years ago in *Planned Parenthood v. Casey*. *Stenberg* is six years old, was a 5 to 4 decision, hasn't been woven into subsequent opinions, and was never reaffirmed. *Roe* affects many women and is popular. *Stenberg* affects fewer women and is less popular.

A Roberts-Alito-Stevens court would probably overturn *Stenberg* in June 2007. There's no chance it would overturn *Roe*, since five of the justices who reaffirmed *Roe* in *Casey* would still be on the court. But the ruling could set off a political explosion. That's what happened 17 years ago when the court, in *Webster v. Reproductive Health Services*, narrowed its interpretation of *Roe*. Justice Harry Blackmun, *Roe*'s author, warned the country that he would soon have to retire, putting *Roe* in jeopardy. That was enough to scare pro-choice voters and make them a decisive force in many states.

A similar warning from Stevens in the upcoming partial-birth case could easily set off such an explosion next summer. Or Stevens could guarantee such an explosion by retiring.

South Dakota's Law Bans Almost All Abortions

If he does neither, South Dakota will do it for him. Because the South Dakota ban so flagrantly defies *Roe*, lower courts will probably strike it down quickly, moving it up the chain. If it comes out of an appeals court by the end of 2007, abortion-rights groups will take it straight to the high court, hoping to make *Roe* a central issue in the 2008 elections. The court might refuse to hear the case if it's clear that five justices won't reconsider *Roe*. Or it might sit on the case until after the elections. But the explosion will happen anyway. By May 2008, Stevens will be 88, two years beyond the age at which any other recent justice has died or retired. Everyone will know that he has one foot out the door, and so does *Roe*.

In short, 2008 will look a lot like 1989, with a surge of pro-abortion-rights voting and a frightened retreat by anti-abortion politicians. But one thing will be different: The House, Senate and White House will be up for grabs. Instead of picking up a couple of governorships, Democrats and abortion-rights supporters could find themselves in control of the federal government.

That's where they need to ditch their old script. The last time abortion-rights backers were in power over both Congress and the White House, in 1993 and 1994, they tried to

Current Policies Contribute to High Abortion Rates

The White House frequently backs precisely the policies that cause America to have one of the highest abortion rates in the West. Compared with other countries, the U.S. lags in sex education and in availability of contraception—financing for contraception under the Title X program has declined 59 percent in constant dollars since 1980—so we have higher unintended pregnancy rates and abortion rates.

Nicholas D. Kristof, "Beyond Chastity Belts,"
The New York Times, *May 2, 2006.*

enshrine *Roe* in federal law and subsidize abortions through Medicaid and President Bill Clinton's health-insurance proposal. A couple of years ago, in a book about the abortion-rights movement, I suggested that its agenda then had been too ambitious. Now I think it wasn't ambitious enough. Real ambition isn't about fortifying the territory you've won. It's about moving on so that the territory behind you no longer needs defending. The territory we need to leave behind is Roe.

Roe established a right to abortion through the end of the second trimester. The latter part of that time frame has always been the most controversial. Improvements in neonatal care have made fetuses viable—capable of surviving delivery—earlier than was possible in 1973. That's why Justice O'Connor said *Roe* was "on a collision course with itself" and eventually led her colleagues to abandon the trimester framework. Meanwhile, sonograms and embryology have made people aware of how well-developed fetuses are while still legally vulnerable to abortion. We even do surgery on fetuses now, which makes aborting them seem that much more perverse. These developments may explain, in part, why two-thirds of Americans think abortion should be illegal in the second trimester—and why anti-abortion activists targeted partial-birth abortions for legislative assault.

Abortions Can Be Avoided with Contraception

But if medical technology has helped to expose this moral problem, it can also help us solve it. Second-trimester abortions are becoming not just harder to stomach, but easier to avoid. In 1973, according to the Alan Guttmacher Institute, fewer than 40 percent of abortions took place before the ninth week of gestation. By 2000, the latest year for which data have been analyzed, the percentage was nearly 60 and rising. The same high-resolution ultrasound that makes you queasy about aborting a 12-week fetus has made it safer to perform abortions at four or five weeks instead of waiting, as women were once routinely told to do. In 1993, only 7 percent of abortion providers could end a pregnancy at four weeks or earlier; by 2001, 37 percent could do it. And by 2002, two-thirds of clinics belonging to the National Abortion Federation were offering pills that abort pregnancies in the first seven weeks.

Better yet, technology is helping many women avoid unwanted pregnancies altogether. According to the Centers for Disease Control [CDC], "emergency contraception"—high-dose birth-control pills taken after sex to block ovulation, fertilization or implantation—was almost unheard of a decade ago. By 2002, however, about 10 percent of women between the ages of 18 and 24 had used such pills. Some activists are fighting these pills in many states and at the Food and Drug Administration, but polls suggest that even most people who oppose legal abortion would tolerate the pills.

The most widely accepted moral solution, short of abstinence, is contraception taken before sex. Here, the news is basically good: Contraceptive use rose 11 percent from 1982 to

2002 (though progress was uneven), and during this period, the abortion rate dropped by about 30 percent.

Birth Control Is Now More Effective

Birth control isn't just more common; it's more effective. The weak link in contraception is the human being who's too excited, impatient or forgetful to take it or use it carefully. But technology can also help circumvent that weak link. When the CDC began tracking birth-control methods in 1982, it had no category for long-lasting injectable contraceptives or implants. By 2002, it found that 4 percent of women were using these methods. Some injectables require refills every three months, but implants have improved considerably. The maker of Implanon, for instance, says that this implant takes barely a minute to insert, begins working within 24 hours, prevents pregnancy for up to three years and can be removed in less than three minutes with a 90 percent probability that a woman will resume ovulating the next month.

Technology can't avert all our failings or tragedies. There will always be abortions. But when you look at the trends— more foolproof contraception, more access to morning-after pills, earlier and fewer abortions—you can begin to envision a gradual, voluntary exodus from at least half the time frame protected by *Roe*. That's the half the public doesn't support.

Maybe that six-month window made more sense in 1973 than it does today. Maybe, if we spend the next 10 years helping women avoid second-trimester abortions, we won't have to spend the 40 years defending them. Maybe the best way to end the assault on *Roe* is to make it irrelevant.

The road out of *Roe* won't be easy. Conservatives are already fighting early abortion pills, morning-after pills, sex education and birth control. But that's a different fight from the one we've been stuck in since 1973. It's a more winnable fight, and a more righteous one. Five hundred years from now, people will look back on surgical abortions the way we look back on the butchery of medieval barbers. Like the barbers, we're trying to help people to the best of our ability. But our ability is growing. So should our wisdom, and our ambitions.

> *"The gigantic increase in the incidence of abortion and of sexually transmitted infections bears witness to the promiscuity that followed the legalization and wide availability of chemical contraceptives."*

Birth Control Results in More Abortions

Dr. John B. Shea

In the following viewpoint, Dr. John B. Shea argues that contraception has not only led to a greater number of abortions, but has also resulted in an increase in sexually transmitted infections and promiscuity. He contends that contraception greatly dishonors marriage, and that the practice of contraception causes men to lose respect for women, considering them a mere instrument of selfish enjoyment. Shea wrote this article for Catholic Insight.

As you read, consider the following questions:

1. According to Dr. John B. Shea, what has happened because of the extensive use of contraception?
2. Why does the Catholic Church oppose the use of contraception?

Dr. John B. Shea, "What the Church Teaches About Human Reproduction," *Catholic Insight*, September 29, 2006. Copyright 2006 Catholic Insight. Reproduced by permission.

3. How does the Catholic Church feel about artificial reproductive technologies?

The Catholic Church teaches that "the direct interruption of the generative process already begun, and, above all, directly willed and procured abortion, even if for therapeutic reasons, are absolutely excluded as licit means of regulating birth. Equally excluded . . . is direct sterilization, whether perpetual or temporary, whether of the man or the woman."[1]

Contraception Can Be Viewed as Abortion

This teaching prohibits contraception by means of the condom; intrauterine device; vasectomy or tubal ligation; and chemical contraception by the use of oral contraceptives, morning after pills, or the administration of contraceptives by injection or in a skin patch. The reason for this prohibition is that contraception breaks the inseparable connection, willed by God and unable to be broken by man on his own initiative, between the unitive meaning and the procreative meaning of the conjugal act.

Contraception greatly dishonours marriage, the greatness of which is beautifully described by Dietrich von Hildebrand. "No natural human good has been exalted so high in the New Testament. No other good has been chosen to become one of the Seven Sacraments. No other has been endowed with the honor of participating in the establishment of the Kingdom of God. . . . The wonderful, divinely appointed relationship between the mysterious procreation of a new human being, and this most intimate communion of love . . . illuminates the grandeur and solemnity of this union. . . . Thus it is that in order to preserve the reverent attitude of the spouses toward the mystery of this union, this general connection between procreation and the communion of love must always be maintained."[2]

Cause for Concern

History has clearly demonstrated how prescient Pope Paul VI was, when he predicted that the practice of contraception would cause the man to lose respect for the woman, considering her a mere instrument of selfish enjoyment. The gigantic increase in the incidence of abortion and of sexually transmitted infections bears witness to the promiscuity that followed the legalization and wide availability of chemical contraceptives. The Pope also warned of the danger that public authorities, which take no heed of moral exigencies, would try to solve problems of the community by means illicit for married couples. Witness the worldwide promotion of contraception and abortion fostered by the United Nations today; and also, the mandatory one-child policy of the government of China.

Paul VI, in *Humanae vitae*, stated that "If, then, there are serious motives to space out births, which derive from the physical or psychological conditions of husband and wife, or from external conditions, the Church teaches that it is then licit to take into account the natural rhythms immanent in the generative functions, for the use of manage in the infecund periods only, and in this way to regulate births without offending the moral principles which have been recalled earlier."[3] Pius XII taught that unless some serious circumstances arise, spouses are obliged to have children. However, he also teaches that it is moral for the spouses to limit their family size or even to refrain from having children altogether, if they have sufficiently serious reasons. He stated that "There are serious motives, such as those often mentioned in the so-called medical, eugenic, economic, and social 'indications,' that can except for a long time, perhaps even during the whole duration of the marriage, from the positive and obligatory carrying out of the act."[4]

Family Planning

Gaudium et spes teaches that "Among the married couples who thus fulfill their God-given mission, special mention should be made of those who after prudent reflection and common decisions, courageously undertake the proper up-bringing of a large number of children." It also states that it is the duty of the parents, and of them alone, to decide on the number and spacing of children, and that they should take "into consideration their own good and the good of their children already born or yet to come, and ability to read the signs of the times and of their own situation, on the material and spiritual level, and finally, an estimation of the good of the family, of society, and of the Church."[5]

The morally acceptable way for spacing the birth of children is called "Natural Family Planning." One of the best methods is the Creighton (Hilgers) system. The effectiveness rates of this method for avoiding pregnancy have been shown to be 98.8 to 99.5 at the twelfth month of use.[6] This compares favourably to the pill, of which Planned Parenthood's Web site states: "Of 100 women who use the Pill, only 8 will become pregnant during the first year of typical use."

Relevant Medical Facts

Some chemical "contraceptives" abort *all* of the time. All of them abort *some* of the time. They do this by preventing implantation of an embryo in the uterus.[7] Elites in the medical profession try to justify their use of the word "contraceptive" by stating that there is no embryo before implantation. This statement is false. The science of human embryology demonstrated over 100 years ago, that a new individual human being comes into existence when the single cell zygote is formed, either by fertilization or by cloning.[8]

Using the oral contraceptive pill (OCP) before the first child is born causes a 40% increase in the risk of breast cancer. Taking it for four or more years before the first child is born grows that risk to a 72% increase. The OCP also increases the risk of cancer of the cervix of the uterus and of the liver.[9] The condom does not provide complete protection from the risk of acquiring sexually transmitted infection.[10]

Artificial Reproductive Technologies (ART)

A human being is normally brought into existence by the fertilization of an ovum by a sperm. This can be achieved by sexual intercourse, or in the laboratory by in vitro fertilization (IVF). Reproduction of a human being can also be achieved by cloning. There are many different methods of cloning that include nuclear transfer, embryo splitting, etc.

The Church teaches that IVF and human cloning are morally forbidden. Why? IVF between husband and wife is condemned because it is illicit in itself and in opposition to the dignity of procreation and the conjugal union. IVF in which the sperm or ovum of a third person is used, is also condemned, because, in addition, it violates the reciprocal commitment of spouses and shows a grave lack of regard for that essential property of marriage which is unity. It also deprives the child of her or his filial relationship with parental origins, can hinder the maturing of personal identity, can damage personal relationships within the family, and has repercussions on civil society.[11]

IVF is neither in fact achieved nor positively willed as an expression and fruit of a specific act of conjugal union. The human embryo is treated as a product of technology and not as a gift of God. In its use and in the use of many other techniques of genetic engineering, a human person is objectively deprived of his or her proper perfection. Such fertilization establishes the domination of technology over the origin and destiny of the person. This domination is contrary to the dignity and equality that must be common to parents and children. Therefore, IVF and cloning are morally unacceptable.[12]

The Hard Facts

• Few of the children conceived by IVF are ever born. In each cycle, six to eight embryos are conceived. At most, two are implanted. The rest are either disposed of immediately, or are frozen and eventually, most die. Only 25% or those conceived

Still So Many Abortions

We can count at least 15 types of contraception readily available to almost anyone at any time, day or night—and yet we're faced with a staggering rate of abortion. One out of every three pregnancies in this country ends in abortion. According to the above logic, as the availability of contraception has increased we should have seen a dramatic decrease in the numbers of abortions, but 1.3 million abortions a year prove that this logic is fatally flawed. We are only fooling ourselves if we think that widely-available contraception reduces abortion.

Father Thomas J. Euteneuer,
"Does Contraception Really Prevent Abortion?"
Human Life International, March 30, 2007. www.hli.org.

are implanted, and of them, only 20% are born. Therefore, only 5% of IVF embryos are born alive. The Australian bioethicist, Nicholas Tonti-Filippini, calculates that the chance of saving a given frozen human embryo by implantation is less than 2%.[13]

• Birth defects associated with ART: 4.9-7.2 fold increase in malignant tumour of the retina; 5% incidence of Beckwith-Wiedemann Syndrome (large tongue, predisposition to cancer); in Brazil, the incidence of cancer increased 117 times; cerebral palsy increased 1.4-1.7 times; four-fold increase in developmental delay; premature birth increased 5.6 times; low birth rate increased 9.8 times and heart deformity increased 4 times.[14]

• To achieve IVF, a woman is given hormones to stimulate the development of many ova at the same time. This may cause Ovarian Hyper-stimulation Syndrome. Symptoms include nausea, vomiting, and breathing difficulty. In rare cases, blood clots, kidney or lung disease may occur and may be life threatening.

• Dr. Thomas Hilgers' Fertility*Care* System: Dr. Hilgers' Natural Procreative Technology is a method of care that involves precise diagnosis of the hormonal causes of infertility, and its appropriate treatment. It is also morally acceptable as a way to help an infertile woman to conceive, and is two to three times more successful than IVF, at a fraction of the cost. One study on women who had previous failed IVF, showed a success rate of 36.2%. The Hilgers system has been shown to be up to 80% successful in helping women to have a successful pregnancy after they have suffered repeated miscarriages. It cuts the rate of premature birth in half, thus helping to reduce the incidence of brain damage.[15]

Notes

1. Pope Paul VI, Encyclical Letter, *Humanae vitae*, n. 14. 1968.
2. Dietrich von Hildebrand, *Marriage: The mystery of faithful love*, Sophia Institute Press, Manchester, New Hampshire, paperback, 1997. p.3, 27–28.
3. See reference number one.
4. Pius XII, "Address to the Italian Catholic Union of Midwives", (Oct. 29, 1951), in AAS LLIII (1951).
5. *Gaudium et spes*, n. 50.
6. Thomas W. Hilgers, M.D. and Joseph B. Stanford, M.D., M.S.P.H., "Creighton Model NaproProTechnology for Avoiding Pregnancy: Use Effectiveness," *Journal of Reproductive Medicine*, 1998; 43: 495–502.
7. "Birth-Control methods which cause abortion," Society for the Protection of Unborn Children, information@spuc.org.uk.
8. Keith Moore and T.V.N. Persaud, *The Developing Human: Clinically Oriented Embryology*, 6th. edition, Philadelphia: W.B. Saunders Co., 1998, p. 2.
9. Romieu I., Berlin I., et al. Oral Contraceptives and Birth Control. Review and meta-Analysis. Cancer. 1990; 66. 2253–2263.
10. John B. Shea, M.B., B.Ch. *The Safer Sex Illusion*, Life Ethics Information Centre, Toronto.
11. Instruction on Bioethics: *Donum vitae*, Sacred Congregation of the Doctrine of the Faith, 1987.
12. Ibid. n. 5.
13. Nicholas Tonti-Filippini, "The Embryo Rescue Debate," *National Catholic Bioethics Quarterly*, 2003. Spring; 3(1): 111–37.
14. What's Wrong with Assisted Reproductive Technology? Institute of Science in Society, (ISIS). ISIS press release, 03/11/03, www.i-sis.org.uk/wwwART.php.
15. Thomas W. Hilgers, M.D., *The Medical and Surgical Practice of NaProTechnology*, Pope Paul VI Institute Press, Omaha, Nebraska, 2004.

> *"Experts in the fields of pharmacy, biology, gynecology, and obstetrics have come to the conclusion that today's hormonal contraceptives not only possess their contraceptive properties but have potential abortifacient mechanisms that can kick in when the contraceptive mechanism fails."*

Emergency Contraception Is Harmful

Ann Shibler

In the following viewpoint, Ann Shibler argues that many women are being misled about the real nature of emergency contraception, as well as most birth control in general, which she contends are intended to chemically induce abortions. Shibler maintains that supporters of birth control and emergency contraception also are deceiving women by claiming that pregnancy does not begin until five to seven days after conception and not at the moment of fertilization. Ann Shibler, an editorial assistant for the John Birch Society online, wrote this article for The New American.

Ann Shibler, "Growing Debate Over Abortifacients," The *New American*, vol. 24, January 21, 2008, pp. 19–22. Copyright © 2008 American Opinion Publishing Incorporated. Reproduced by permission.

As you read, consider the following questions:

1. According to Ann Shibler, how many surgical abortions have been performed in the United States since 1967?

2. In the author's opinion, what does the decrease in the number of abortions not take into account?

3. According to the author, what does an effective contraceptive do to prevent conception?

Generally speaking, the average American, whether pro-life or pro-abortion, is aware that the number of abortions committed in this country is in the millions. Both the Center for Disease Control (CDC) and the Alan Guttmacher Institute (AGI), an arm of Planned Parenthood (PP), keep count by directly surveying doctors and clinics for the data each year. According to records they've compiled since 1967, when some individual states decriminalized abortion, an estimated 46 million surgical abortions have taken place in the United States. That's an average of 1.3 million innocent lives terminated per year.

AGI reports that the number of abortions has been decreasing in recent years, from 1.36 million in 1996 to 1.29 million by 2002, with that trend continuing downward through 2005. However, these numbers don't account for chemically induced, sometimes called medically induced, abortions, which are now on the rise.

Whether termed "abortifacients," "emergency contraceptives," or the "morning after pill," these are drugs designed to prohibit a newly conceived child from implanting in the womb for nourishment and are now widely available, with statistical use largely unreported. RU-486 (Mifepristone), methotrexate, and the Intra-uterine Device (IUD) all prevent the fertilized embryo's implantation, with Mifepriston and methotrexate also causing the fetus to be expelled. Some injections produce the same effect. The World Health Organization's newest "vaccines" make a woman's immune system attack and destroy her own baby.

But the main abortion-inducing drug just may be birth control pills (BCPs). Experts in the fields of pharmacy, biology, gynecology, and obstetrics have come to the conclusion that today's hormonal contraceptives not only possess their contraceptive properties but have potential abortifacient mechanisms that can kick in when the contraceptive mechanism fails. Though these claims are backed up with scientific evidence, contraceptive users may be innocently ignorant about the true properties of these substances.

Women Should Know That Emergency Contraception Causes Abortions

Few prescribing physicians and patients seem to be aware of the postfertilization effects of birth control pills. This lack of understanding represents a failure to fully inform patients about something with physical, moral, ethical, and psychological consequences.

In the *Archives of Family Medicine*, an out-of-print journal published by the American Medical Association, Drs. Walter L. Larimore and Joseph B. Stanford, in a 2000 paper entitled "Postfertilization Effects of Oral Contraceptives and Their Relationship to Informed Consent," advocate for objective presentation of the potential for the abortifacient or postfertilization effects to all patients during informed-consent discussions. They propose that failure to disclose this information might violate the morals of some women and "would effectively eliminate the likelihood that the woman's consent was truly informed." They note that women who did not have full disclosure or understanding might learn of the abortifacient effect after taking BCPs and respond with "disappointment, anger, guilt, sadness, rage, depression, or a sense of having been violated by the provider."

So, why hasn't the proper and credible information been disclosed to patients? What about physicians, nurses, counselors, and religious pastors? Why have they been silent in this matter? For one thing, obscure technical and scientific journals are not everyday reading for most. The dilemma is perhaps furthered by the medical textbooks used in universities that do not.

Experts in the fields of pharmacy, biology, distinguish between contraceptives and abortifacients—most doctors have simply never heard of it before, adding to the confusion.

Untrue Claims That Conception Doesn't Begin at Fertilization

However, there is another reason why there's no clear understanding about what could be the lethal consequences of BCPs—outright deception. In the mid-60s, the American College of Obstetricians, with the agreement of the CDC and Department of Health, Education and Welfare, along with Big Pharma, adopted a new definition of pregnancy. Previously it had been defined as beginning from the moment of fertilization—conception. They redefined it, claiming pregnancy did not start until the baby is implanted in the lining of the womb usually occurring five to seven days after conception. With this "new" definition, the abortifacient purveyors can, through semantic manipulation, openly promote abortifacients as contraceptives, hoodwinking overworked physicians and busy women alike.

According to definition, an effective contraceptive would absolutely prevent conception—it would suppress or inhibit ovulation, making it impossible for sperm to meet with eggs. The only products falling into this category are jellies and foams—spermicides—and condoms. (Diaphragms are considered a mechanical barrier and not true contraceptives. But they are not abortifacients either.)

Today's birth control pills are not the same "Pill" of the 1960s. That first pill with its high dose of hormones did prevent ovulation in the majority (but not all) of its users, and conception. In the mid-70s, because of the dangerous side effects associated with the high-dose "Pill," the pharmaceutical companies started reducing the doses of the hormones estrogen and progestin from 150 micrograms down to 35 micrograms by 1988. Now some are as low as 20 micrograms.

Birth Control Is Chemical Abortion

BCPs today work in one of three ways: by suppressing or inhibiting ovulation so that fertilization is impeded; altering cervical mucus to reduce sperm migration; or via a backup mechanism that prevents implantation of the newly conceived human life in the lining of the womb by creating a chemically hostile environment, sometimes called a post-fertilization effect. In 1994, Dr. Thomas Hilgers, a respected fertility specialist and clinical professor in the Department of Obstetrics and Gynecology at Creighton University School of Medicine, said "All birth control pills available have a mechanism which disturbs or disintegrates the lining of the uterus to the extent that the possibility of abortion exists when break-through ovulation occurs." (Break-through ovulation is the term used when the contraceptive component of the Pill has failed, allowing ovulation and therefore conception to take place.)

Pharmaceutical company statements, medical textbooks, doctors, scientists, and even the government show total agreement when it comes to the abortifacient nature of the backup mechanism. Dr. Leon Speroff, the nation's premier contraceptive expert and advocate, in his paper "A Clinical Guide for Contraception," says about BCPs, "The progestin in the combination pill produces an endometrium which is not receptive to ovum implantation, a decidualized bed with exhausted and atrophied glands." Dutch gynecologist Dr. Nine Van Der Vange of the Society for Advancement in Contraception said, "The

A Fetus Is a Human Life

A human life is not a disease like cancer of the uterus, where the law of double effect might justify the performance of a hysterectomy, despite the indirect and unintended death of a fetus. The embryo did come into existence as the result of a violent and unjust act, the mother's rape, but her or his very existence is not an injustice in itself. To kill such an unborn child would simply add the sin and injustice of murder to the sin and injustice of rape.

J.B. Shea, "The 'Morning-After' Pill," Catholic Insight, *May 2004.*

contraceptive preparations are more complex than has been thought. They are not only based on inhibition of ovulation."

Searle, Ortho, and Wyeth-Ayerst, major manufacturers of BCPs, admit in the fine print of some of their package inserts that alterations in the endometrium (uterine lining) reduce the likelihood of "implantation" of the already conceived embryo. Wyeth-Ayerst says its product maximizes protection "by causing endometrial changes that will not support implantation." The Food and Drug Administration reported as early as 1976 that the Pill changed "the characteristics of the uterus so that it is not receptive to a fertilized egg." And a standard medical reference, Danforth's Obstetrics and Gynecology, states, "The production of glycogen by the endometrial glands is diminished by the ingestion of oral contraceptives, which impairs the survival of the blastocyst in the uterine cavity." A blastocyst refers to a newly conceived human being.

While it is difficult to quantify the postfertilization effects of BCPs due to the failure of the contraceptive component, there is scientific research available to support the thesis that chemically induced abortions are probable. Dr. Van Der Vange conducted an award-winning study and showed, from research based on ultrasound exams and hormonal indicators, a 4.7 percent rate of breakthrough ovulation occurring in women who were given high-dose pills. Dr. Don Gambrell, Jr., a gynecological endocrinologist at the Medical College of Georgia in Augusta, noted a 14-percent incidence of breakthrough ovulation in women taking the relatively low dose 50-microgram BCPs in his research. Of course, the greater the rate of breakthrough ovulation, the greater the chance that the postfertilization mechanism would kick in to end the pregnancy.

Dr. Bogomir M. Kuhar, a doctor of pharmacy and director of Pharmacists for Life International, cited numerous studies by experts and pharmaceutical companies in his paper, "Infant Homicides Through Contraception." Dr. Kuhar concluded that the average rate of breakthrough ovulation due to a number of factors is between 2 percent and 10 percent per cycle. By factoring in a 25 percent overall conception rate for normally fertile couples per cycle with a user estimate of 13.9 million (Kuhar's article was written in 1993 so the user estimate might be lower than today's), and multiplying them, he deduced a 2 percent rate would yield the potential for 69,500 chemical abortions per cycle or 834,000 per year, while the 10 percent rate would yield 347,500 per cycle or 4,171,000 chemical abortions per year—almost all of them due to the Pill's abortifacient mechanisms. (Other factors such as naturally occurring miscarriages and surprise pregnancies would have some impact on the numbers.)

More Chemical Abortions than Surgical Abortions

The longer-lasting (three months) Depo-Provera injection acts by altering the lining of the uterus, preventing implantation of the newly conceived life. Based on one million users with an ovulation rate of 40 to 60 percent, combined with a 25 percent conception rate, yields either 1.2 million chemical abortions per year, or on the higher end, 1.8 million a year. The popular Norplant, a subdermal implant of six tiny rods containing only progestin, acts up to five years as an abortifacient. With an ovulation rate of 50 to 60 percent, 2,250,000 to 2,925,000 chemical abortions might be the result.

The newer "mini-pill" uses only progestin as well, and is often given to postpartum women who are nursing their babies. Ovulation is estimated at taking place 67 to 81 percent of the time, making the possibility of postfertilization effects high.

One thing is certain: there is no data that denies the existence of a potential post-conceptional effect; it simply cannot be ruled out. And there is evidence concerning a causal link between hormonal birth control and abortion, but nothing definitive. With the approval of RU-486 and methotrexate, both "morning after" drugs that kill the unborn swiftly and mercilessly, plus all 44 varieties of BCPs, implantable and injectable-style drugs, and the new "vaccines," the number of surgical abortions could now pale in comparison to the chemically aborted.

For the pro-life crowd that works so tirelessly in trying to persuade women not to have a single surgical abortion, the evidence supporting chemical abortions should prove that more work needs to be done.

> *"Since emergency contraception has been made available in nonprescription form in France, over 1.5 million treatments have been dispensed, 97% with no prescription. As a result, France has an extremely low abortion rate."*

Emergency Contraception Is Not Harmful

Jesse Mesich

In the following viewpoint, Jesse Mesich argues that the United States should follow the lead of other countries in allowing women access to emergency contraception without a prescription. Citing data from other countries, Mesich maintains that doing so would not only lead to a reduction in the number of abortions, but would also help women avoid pharmacists who refuse to fill such prescriptions. Jesse Mesich is an intern at the National Organization for Women (NOW) Foundation.

As you read, consider the following questions:

1. According to a study cited by Jesse Mesich, by what percentage would abortions be reduced if emergency contraception could be dispensed without a prescription?

Jesse Mesich, "Emergency Contraception: U.S. Out of Step," *National Organization for Women*, October 26, 2005. Reprinted with permission of the National Organization for Women.

2. What kind of policies do South Dakota, Arkansas, Mississippi, and Georgia have regarding a pharmacist's right to refuse to fill a prescription, according to the author?

3. Why did two officials from the Food and Drug Administration resign their positions, according to Mesich?

The Food and Drug Administration's [FDA] unwarranted delay in approving over-the-counter (OTC) sale of emergency contraception (EC) has been much in the news lately. Against the advice of two FDA advisory committees and contrary to the endorsement of some 70 respected medical associations, several FDA officials have suggested that availability of EC to women age 16 and under would lead to promiscuity. There is no evidence that EC use by adolescents increases their level of sexual activity, and there is specific evidence that it does not. Many close observers believe that this fallacious assertion is pandering to the [George W. Bush] administration's extremist anti-birth control activists.

A 2001 study conducted by the Alan Guttmacher Institute concluded that emergency contraception, if readily dispensed, could cause a 43% reduction of the approximate 1.37 million abortions that occur each year in this country. If EC was dispensed OTC worldwide, it would dramatically cut the approximately 46 million abortions worldwide each year. Of the 210 million women around the globe who become pregnant each year, about 80 million of their pregnancies are unplanned, according to the Center for Reproductive Rights.

Opponents of EC often assert that prohibiting a fertilized ovum from implantation in the uterus, which sometimes happens with EC use, is tantamount to an abortion. While this debate drags on in the U.S., millions of women are denied easier access to a proven safe drug that is available to women in many other countries.

Fewer Abortions Overseas with Over-the-Counter EC

Many other nations not only have EC available in prescription form, but also provide it over the counter [OTC]. Around the globe, there are approximately 39 countries that facilitate access to EC without prescription, including: Albania, Belgium, Canada, Denmark, Finland, France, India, Israel, Morocco, Norway, Portugal, Republic of Congo, South Africa, Sweden, and the United Kingdom.

One of the countries that provides emergency contraception without a prescription is France, where it has been available since the 1970s. In May of 1999, it was packaged specifically as the "morning-after pill." One month later, France made EC a nonprescription drug, allowing women to get it directly from the pharmacist as France does not have over-the-counter drugs like in the U.S. The French government also reimburses over 65% of the cost of the drug, and minors are allowed to receive it free of cost and without parental notification. Furthermore, since December 2000, minors have been able to receive EC from their high school nurses. Since EC has been made available in nonprescription form in France, over 1.5 million treatments have been dispensed, 97% with no prescription. As a result, France has an extremely low abortion rate.

India is the latest country to allow EC OTC. The Indian Health Minister announced on August 31 that his country had approved the sale of emergency contraception over-the-counter, and expressed hope that allowing EC OTC will reduce the number of unsafe abortions in India, which kill 20,000 women annually. The health minister said that having the emergency contraception available without prescription would be important in alleviating women's distress about seeing a doctor for this reason.

Some States Are Blocking Easier Access to EC

It is not only foreign countries that see the practicality in providing emergency contraception over-the-counter; a few U.S. states have also made access easier. In 1988, Washington was the first state to allow women to get EC directly from a pharmacist, without first going to a doctor. This pilot plan was based on a collaboration between doctors and pharmacies that set specific screening criteria women must meet in order to receive EC. There were almost 35,600 prescriptions filled for EC from February 1998 until the trial expired in June 2001, preventing thousands of unwanted pregnancies. Washington's pilot program opened the door for other states to explore their own EC OTC policies. Currently, Hawaii and Alaska allow EC to be sold OTC using the Washington model of collaboration between doctors and pharmacists. Additionally, California, Maine, and New Mexico allow EC to be sold OTC through their specific state-approved protocol. Two other states, Massachusetts and New Hampshire, have also passed laws allowing easier access to EC, however, they are still trying to implement them.

Massachusetts is the most recent state to pass legislation allowing EC to be sold over the counter. The bill initially sailed through the state's Senate and House of Representatives and passed overwhelmingly. However, Massachusetts Governor Mitt Romney vetoed the bill on July 29 [2005] in keeping with (he claimed) his campaign pledge not to change any state "abortion laws." Legislators were able to override the veto on September 15 of [2005], thus enacting the law. The Massachusetts law is based on the Washington state legislation, and also guarantees that emergency rooms will offer EC to rape victims.

Despite these advances by the states in dispensing EC OTC, there is also a counter-movement by pharmacists who are refusing to fill prescriptions for EC and even for birth control

Fewer Pregnancies and Abortions with EC

To opponents of Plan B, who worry that easy access might increase sexual promiscuity and that teenagers should have clinical supervision, Wayne Shields, ARHP [Association of Reproductive Health Professionals] president responded: "These arguments . . . are red herrings. In fact, countries that allow OTC access to EC (emergency contraception) and offer comprehensive sex and sexuality education have far lower rates of teen pregnancy and abortion than we do. It's a no-brainer."

Ruth Rosen, "The Politics of Contraception,"
San Francisco Chronicle, *May 13, 2004.*

pills. These pharmacists claim moral or religious objections to filling the prescriptions and, therefore, refuse to fill them even though their female customers received their prescriptions from a doctor. This recent campaign has been instigated by a number of well-known anti-abortion rights organizations and political religious organizations.

More Pharmacists Refuse to Fill Prescriptions

The Alan Guttmacher Institute reports that during a six month period in 2004 more than 180 pharmacists refused to fill prescriptions for EC. In fact, four states—South Dakota, Arkansas, Mississippi, and Georgia—have policies that allow pharmacists to refuse to dispense a prescription if they personally disagree with the practice. What is even more alarming is that eight more states are considering similar legislation. We must counter this alarming trend that threatens to deny effective and needed medicine to women.

This decision by individual pharmacists to limit women's reproductive rights has brought outrage from many quarters. Supporters of over-the-counter EC have lobbied legislatures to ensure availability through mandated pharmacist referrals and other means. Two states, Illinois and Nevada, have laws ensuring a patient's access to this legally-prescribed medicine by making it illegal for a pharmacy to refuse to fill a prescription for EC. Five additional states and the U.S. Congress have had similar bills introduced. The federal bill is H.R. 1539, sponsored by Rep. Carolyn McCarthy (D-N.Y.), which stipulates that if a pharmacist refuses to fill a prescription, the pharmacy must arrange to have another pharmacist fill the prescription within four hours of the initial refusal. One of the important advantages of over-the-counter availability is that it would completely bypass pharmacists' refusals. Perhaps that is why right-wing, anti-birth control activists are fighting so hard to stop EC OTC.

The Food and Drug Administration's foot-dragging has prompted several officials to speak out. Two top FDA officials: Dr. Susan F. Wood, who was assistant commissioner for Women's Health and director of the FDA's Office of Women's Health, and Dr. Frank Davidoff, who was a consultant to the FDA's Nonprescriptive Drug Committee, have stepped-down from their respective positions in protest of the government's delay in providing EC to the women of this country. Davidoff voiced this frustration in his letter of resignation: "I can no longer associate myself with an organization that is capable of making such an important decision so flagrantly on the basis of political influence, rather than the scientific and clinical evidence."

Furthermore, many in Congress are becoming increasingly more frustrated with the delayed FDA ruling and growing reports of pharmacist refusal. On October 7 [2005], a bipartisan letter was sent to the FDA Acting Commissioner Andrew von

Eschenbach urging him to stop the delay and allow EC to be sold over the counter to all women.

Educate Women About EC

Another challenge for women's reproductive rights advocates lies in what appears to be a significant gap in public awareness. A 2003 poll conducted by the Kaiser Family Foundation revealed that 32% of women aged 18–44 were not aware that there is a method of contraception that is effective after unprotected intercourse has already occurred. Additionally, only 6% of women have ever used EC. A successful educational campaign about what emergency contraception is and how it works, as well as information about the need for EC availability without prescription, would help immensely. Also, when EC is made available over-the-counter in the U.S., there must be an education campaign to ensure that women—especially young women—know about this safe and effective contraceptive option.

Periodical Bibliography

The following articles have been selected to supplement the diverse views presented in this chapter.

Colleen Boland Toder   "Prevention First?" *Human Life Review*, Winter 2007.

Jo Carlowe   "Behind the Headlines: Can Emergency Pill Stem Abortion?" *GP*, September 29, 2006.

Judith Davidoff   "Now It's the Pill They're After: Right-to-Life Movement Calls It Chemical Abortion," *The Capital Times*, August 1, 2005.

Judith Graham   "Abortion Foes' New Rallying Point: Conservatives Take on Contraception," *Chicago Tribune*, September 24, 2006.

Henry Mark Holzer   "From Condoms to Abortion: *Griswold to Roe*," The Conservative Voice, January 22, 2007. the conservativevoice.com.

William F. Jasper   "Plan B: The George and Hillary Plan," *The New American*, September 18, 2006.

Cristina Page   "The War Against Sex," TomPaine.com, May 17, 2006, tompaine.com.

Shira Saperstein   "Honoring Mrs. Griswold—'No Delays, No Hassles, No Lectures,'" Center for American Progress, June 6, 2005.

Reena Singh   "New Barriers to Emergency Contraception Access for Rape Victims: A Report from Connecticut," *Women's Health Activist*, May-June 2007.

Joshua Zeitz   "*Roe v. Wade*: Finding the Right to Privacy," *American Heritage*, January 22, 2008.

OPPOSING
VIEWPOINTS®
SERIES

CHAPTER 2

Who Should Control Access to Birth Control?

Chapter Preface

In the battle to decide who should have access to birth control, deliberate actions have been taken to either increase its availability or make it less accessible.

A growing number of states have either introduced or passed legislation that deals with conscience clauses and the ability to obtain birth control or emergency contraception. In Arkansas, Georgia, Mississippi, and South Dakota, for example, pharmacists can refuse to fill emergency contraception prescriptions, while New Jersey's law states that pharmacists cannot refuse to dispense a prescription based on ethical, moral, or religious grounds. Illinois Governor Rod Blagojevich signed an emergency order that requires all legal birth control prescriptions to be filled promptly by any pharmacy in Illinois that sells contraceptives. In 2004, it became a law in Illinois that all private insurance companies must cover all birth control devices and services that have been approved by the U.S. Food and Drug Administration (FDA).

Legislation on the federal level has been introduced and then referred back to committee without becoming a law. The Access to Birth Control Act was introduced in Congress in June 2007 to guarantee that a pharmacy would have to fill a legal prescription even if a pharmacist objects to filling it on religious or moral grounds. The act states that the prescription must be filled by another pharmacist who does not object to the prescription and that drug be ordered promptly if it's normally carried by the pharmacy and is out of stock. This legislation was written after the Access to Legal Pharmaceuticals Act, which was introduced in 2005, was sent back to committee. It, too, would have ensured that a pharmacist could not decline to fill a prescription.

When the Deficit Reduction Act of 2005 went into effect in January 2007, limits were placed on how much of a discount pharmaceutical companies could offer for medicine. It was Congress's intention to stop these companies from selling medicine for less than the medicine was being sold under Medicaid. (Medicaid is a government program for low-income families and individuals who meet a specific eligibility requirement. It is administered by the states. Each person may have to pay a copayment but the doctor receives the bulk of his payment directly from the government.)

However, because of this act, college and family-planning clinics were no longer allowed to sell discounted birth control pills, which meant that college students and low-income women were not able to purchase this contraception at an affordable price. Some college and family-planning clinics were able to hoard enough oral contraception so they could continue to offer it at reduced price. Other college clinics decided to stop carrying birth control pills completely.

A 2006 National College Health Assessment survey by the American College Health Association (ACHA) found that 39 percent of female college students said they had used birth control pills.

A bill was introduced in Congress in November 2007 that would have restored the discounted prices for oral contraception that had been provided at college and family-planning clinics. It has been referred back to committee for further study.

In the following chapter, the authors examine what should be the extent of government's role when a woman's need to obtain birth control clashes with another person's personal beliefs.

> *"Abstinence-only-until-marriage pro-grams are not only dispensing medical inaccuracies, they have also been shown to be ineffective—and even dangerous."*

The Government Should Fund Comprehensive Sex Education Programs

Eleanor Levie

Eleanor Levie serves on the National Council of Jewish Women (NCJW) as a national board member and is chair of the NCJW's Pennsylvania Public Affairs Committee. In the following view-point, she contends that comprehensive sex education programs, which include information about contraception, should be taught in schools. Levie is critical of abstinence-only sex education, which she believes is unrealistic and misleading. She argues that it is unrealistic because it promotes abstinence as the only ac-ceptable behavior before marriage, and that is misleading be-cause it teaches students, for example, that condoms do nothing to help reduce the number of sexually transmitted diseases (STDs).

Eleanor Levie, "The Right Is Wrong About Sex Education," *The Philadelphia Jewish Voice*, September 2007. Copyright © 2007 *The Philadelphia Jewish Voice*. Reproduced by permission.

As you read, consider the following questions:

1. According to Eleanor Levie, whose needs are being ignored when abstinence-only programs are taught in schools?
2. What is the name of the program that offers an abstinence-only presentation and includes religious ideas and language, according to the author?
3. What would the REAL (Responsible Education About Life) Act do?

It is back to school time, and at far too many public secondary schools, that means it is also back to the dark ages of promoting ignorance and religious rhetoric instead of factual information about human sexuality. In many pockets of Pennsylvania, as in the nation, schools are failing our teens. Failing to provide accurate information about life. Failing to keep them safe from AIDS and other sexually transmitted diseases (STDs). Failing to teach comprehensive sexuality education.

Concerned teachers and parents whisper horror stories—always on conditions of anonymity. A teacher from Philadelphia where middle school students are overwhelmingly poor, African American, and reading below grade level, spoke about girls offering oral sex for a dollar, at the movies and even on the playground. Affluent kids reading at or above grade level may be just as likely to fall victim to ignorance and peer pressure. One suburban mother told of her 13-year-old son confiding of bar mitzvah party "gifts" of oral sex, and relaying his own personal misconceptions, such as "taking daily showers will keep me safe from STDs."

Governmental Sanctions

Is it any wonder adolescents lack the information they need to make wise decisions about their lives? More than one billion dollars in federal funding—$176 million in 2006 alone—have been doled out for abstinence-only-until-marriage programs.

In contrast, there has never been any federal funding stream at all for comprehensive sex education.

President [George W.] Bush and a minority from the extreme religious right are staunch defenders of abstinence as the only acceptable form of behavior outside of marriage—for people of any age. The programs they support promote ignorance over science and prohibit teachers from providing any information about contraception, except for discussing failure rates. American youngsters participating in federally funded abstinence-only programs have been fed fallacies galore, such as:

- "Abortion can lead to suicide."

- "10 percent of women become sterile after an abortion."

- "Touching a person's genitals can result in pregnancy."

- "Condoms do not help stop the spread of STDs."

- "Half the gay male teenagers in the United States have tested positive for the AIDS virus."

Practically ignored by such programs are the needs of kids who are or have been sexually active; one teacher advised such a student to "renew their virginity." Ignored are the needs of students who are, or have been, the victims of sexual violence. Ignored are the needs of gay, lesbian, bisexual, transgendered students, and those questioning their sexual identities.

Religious Rhetoric

For any progressive outraged about the intrusion and imposition of one set of religious beliefs in public schools, the picture is even worse. Many abstinence-only-until-marriage programs currently funded by the federal government and taught in public schools use messages about abstinence that are couched in religious beliefs, including assumptions of when life begins. The Silver Ring Thing, which has received more

Distorted Lessons About Sex

Experts in sex education and AIDS prevention say that in a country where the vast majority of people lose their virginity before their wedding night, these lessons aren't just distorted, they're dangerous. "To promote abstinence-only in the era of AIDS is to promote ignorance. It's inexplicable," says James Wagoner, president of Advocates for Youth, a nonprofit organization devoted to sex education. Some abstinence-only programs, like more comprehensive sex education, have been shown to delay the age at which teenagers first have sex—which almost everyone agrees is a good thing. Yet studies also show that when teenagers from abstinence-only programs do have sex, they're less likely than others to use protection. Perhaps that's why the teen pregnancy rate in Texas remains one of the highest in the country, despite the abstinence-only policies Bush pushed as governor.

Michelle Goldberg, "Bush's Sex Fantasy,"
Salon.com, February 24, 2004. www.salon.com.

than $1 million from the government over the last few years, conducts a nationwide touring program that features a 3-hour "abstinence-only" presentation with prominent religious themes and rhetoric, including the following passage from the New Testament.

> *For this is the will of God, even your sanctification, that ye should abstain from fornication: that each of you know how to possess his own vessel in sanctification and honor. . . .*

Abstinence-only-until-marriage programs are not only dispensing medical inaccuracies, they have also been shown to be ineffective—and even dangerous. All the major medical, public health research groups and institutions—the American

Medical Association, the American Academy of Pediatrics, the American Nurses Association, the American College of Obstetricians and Gynecologists, the American Psychological Association, the American Public Health Association, the National Institutes of Health, and the Institute of Medicine—support comprehensive sexuality education.

Who does not remember when Senator Bill Frist, a former medical doctor serving as Majority Leader of the Senate, was unwilling to dispute the notion that AIDS can be spread via sweat and tears. On the other side of the Capitol, Congressman Henry Waxman (D-CA) has actively exposed the flaws and dangers of abstinence-only curricula. Reports issued in 2004 from his office found that 80 percent of the programs studied included distorted information. Waxman has repeatedly warned that, "Something is seriously wrong when federal tax dollars are being used to mislead kids about basic health facts."

NGOs Say No to Abstinence Only

Leading the Jewish community in the fight for age appropriate, medically accurate sex education is the National Council of Jewish Women (NCJW). It has launched Plan A: NCJW's Campaign for Contraceptive Access. As a volunteer organization inspired by Jewish values, NCJW defends religious freedom and the wall separating religion and state. NCJW President Phyllis Snyder speaks out against "small but powerful minority that is attempting to impose a single religious belief on us all ... (in) a climate where—time and again—ideology and politics trump sound science and medicine." Plan A details the impact that can be felt in homes, pharmacies, and doctors' offices, as well as public schools.

NCJW members often work in coalition with other organizations with national scope and grassroots activists. The ACLU [American Civil Liberties Union], People for the American Way, SIECUS—the Sexuality Information and Education

Council of the United States, and Planned Parenthood are all advocating for comprehensive sex education. Here in Pennsylvania, NCJW and other progressive organizations work together through PARSE: Pennsylvanians for Responsible Sex Education.

Good News Ahead?

In one of the last votes in the House before the August [2007] recess, the U.S. House of Representatives attached some conditions to Title V of the Social Security Act that would require that any funded program be proven effective at decreasing teen pregnancy, STD, and HIV/AIDS rates. This was part of the reauthorization of the State Children's Health Insurance Program (SCHIP), set to expire on September 30. Should the Senate approve this bill, and the President sign it into law, much of the decision-making will be given over to the state legislatures.

Clearly, we all need to go back to school. Parents of school age children need to find out what is being taught to their children. Does the program provide age-appropriate, medically accurate information? Is the teacher certified and qualified to teach sex education without mixing personal "pro-choice" or "pro-life" ideology or religious rhetoric? Does the teacher also encourage family communication about sexuality, and help young people with their negotiation skills? Principals need to think long and hard before relegating sex education to whatever gym teachers happen to be available. Federal legislators need to become educated about the Responsible Education About Life, or REAL Act, which would provide federal funds for comprehensive sex education. State legislators need to devote funding to accredited programs, certification standards and curriculum oversight. It all comes down to getting young people the information they need and have a right to, information to help them make wise decisions. In today's world, teenagers cannot afford a failing grade for sex education.

> "Out of 942 total pages of curriculum text reviewed from 9 different 'comprehensive' sex ed curricula, not a single sentence was found urging teens to abstain from sexual activity through high school."

The Government Should Fund Sex Education Programs That Emphasize Abstinence

Melissa G. Pardue

In the following viewpoint, Melissa Pardue argues that abstinence-only sex education programs are effective and are supported by parents and teenagers. She contends that "abstinence-plus" programs emphasize contraception and safe sex and do not really focus on abstinence at all. Pardue, a policy analyst in domestic policy studies at the Heritage Foundation, cites a study about fifth- and sixth-grade girls who participate in the abstinence education program Best Friends. According to the study, these girls are not only more likely to abstain from sex, but are also less likely to use drugs, smoke cigarettes, or drink alcohol. Pardue wrote this article for the Heritage Foundation.

Melissa G. Pardue, "More Evidence of the Effectiveness of Abstinence Education Programs," *The Heritage Foundation*, May 5, 2005. Copyright © 2005 The Heritage Foundation. Reproduced by permission.

As you read, consider the following questions:

1. What does the Best Friends curriculum include and for which grades, according to the author?

2. What did a majority of teenagers in a 2004 National Campaign to Prevent Teen Pregnancy poll report about their feelings about having sex?

3. According to the author, how much did the government spend in 2002 to promote safe sex and contraception programs and how much on abstinence education?

The harmful effects of early sexual activity are well documented. They include sexually transmitted diseases, teen pregnancy, and out-of-wedlock childbearing. As well, teen sexual activity is linked to emotional problems, such as depression, and increased risk of suicide. Abstinence education programs, which encourage teens to delay the onset of sexual activity, are effective in curbing such problems. Opponents of abstinence education, however, claim that abstinence programs don't work and that there has been "no scientific evidence that abstinence programs are effective." New research proves abstinence education opponents wrong once again.

A new study by Dr. Robert Lerner published in the Institute for Youth Development's peer-reviewed journal *Adolescent & Family Health* bolsters the case for the effectiveness of abstinence programs in reducing teens' high-risk behaviors, including sexual activity, smoking, and alcohol and drug use. The study evaluates the effectiveness of the Best Friends abstinence education program and finds that students in it are significantly less likely than their peers to engage in any of these high-risk behaviors. This important research joins ten other evaluations that have also showed positive effects of abstinence programs.

Abstinence Reduces Dangerous Behaviors

According to the study, released in April 2005, junior-high and middle school-aged girls who participated in the Best Friends program, when compared to their peers who did not participate, were:

- Six-and-a-half times more likely to remain sexually abstinent;

- Nearly two times more likely to abstain from drinking alcohol;

- Eight times more likely to abstain from drug use; and

- Over two times more likely to refrain from smoking.

The Best Friends program began in 1987 and currently operates in more than 100 schools across the United States. Its curriculum consists of a character-building program for girls in the fifth or sixth grade, including at least 110 hours of instruction, mentoring, and group activities throughout the year. Discussion topics include friendship, love and dating, self-respect, decision-making, alcohol abuse, drug abuse, physical fitness and nutrition, and AIDS/STDs. The predominant theme of the curriculum is encouragement to abstain from high-risk behavior, including sexual activity. A companion program for boys, Best Men, began in 2000.

When girls who participate in the Best Friends program reach the ninth grade, they have the have the opportunity to enter the Diamond Girls Leadership program, which is designed to help girls maintain their commitment to abstinence. The Diamond Girls program offers opportunities to participate in a jazz choir or dance troupe, which help to foster discipline and social and presentation skills for the future.

According to the Lerner Study, the Best Friends program has been highly effective in reaching its goals. The study compared several years of data on girls from Washington, D.C., who participated in the Best Friends program with data on

Washington, D.C., girls of the same age from the Centers for Disease Control's (CDC) Youth Risk Behavior Survey (YRBS).

Using multiple logistic regressions, which controlled for grade, age, race, and survey year, the study found a significant decrease in the incidence of high-risk behaviors among Best Friends girls as compared to YRBS girls. Specifically, girls who participated the Best Friends program had:

- A 52 percent reduction in the likelihood that they would smoke;

- A 90 percent reduction in the likelihood that they would use drugs;

- A 60 percent reduction in the likelihood that they would drink alcohol; and

- An 80 percent reduction in the likelihood that they would have sex.

Other peer-reviewed studies have also found abstinence programs to be effective in reducing teen pregnancy and teen birthrates. An April 2003 study in *Adolescent & Family Health* found that increased abstinence among 15- to 19-year-old teens accounted for at least two-thirds (67 percent) of the drop in teen pregnancy rates. Increased abstinence also accounted for more than half (51 percent) of the decline in teen birthrates.

The Public Supports Abstinence

An August 2004 study in the *Journal of Adolescent Health* found similar results: 53 percent of the decline in teen pregnancy rates can be attributed to decreased sexual experience among teens aged 15–17 years old, while only 47 percent of the decline is attributed to increased use of contraception among teens.

Not surprisingly, parents overwhelmingly support the abstinence message. A December 2003 Zogby poll found that the overwhelming majority of parents—91 percent—want schools to teach that adolescents should be expected to abstain from sexual activity during high school years. Only 7 percent of parents believe that it is okay for teens in high school to engage in sexual intercourse as long as they use condoms, which is the predominant theme of "comprehensive" sex education.

Teens themselves welcome the abstinence message and appear to be heeding it. A December 2004 poll by the National Campaign to Prevent Teen Pregnancy found that a clear majority of adolescents—69 percent—agree that it is *not* okay for high school teens to engage in sexual intercourse. Data from the CDC confirms this, as the YRBS survey shows that the number of teens who have ever had sexual intercourse has fallen 7 percent in the last 12 years, from 54 percent in 1991 to 46 percent in 2003.

Regrettably, groups like the Sexuality Information and Education Council of the United States (SIECUS) and Advocates for Youth would like to see abstinence programs eliminated and replaced with "comprehensive" sex education. These "comprehensive" programs are often misleadingly labeled "abstinence-plus" and falsely claim to be the middle ground between abstinence and safe sex education. This is not true. These programs are virtually all "plus" and almost no abstinence.

Comprehensive Sex Ed Doesn't Include Abstinence

Analysis of "comprehensive" sex ed programs reveals that these curricula contain little if any meaningful abstinence message. On average, these curricula devote about 4 percent of their content to abstinence. Out of 942 total pages of curriculum text reviewed from 9 different "comprehensive" sex ed curricula, *not a single sentence,* was found urging teens to abstain from sexual activity through high school. The over-

Comprehensive Sex Ed Is Inappropriate for Teens

The U.S. Department of Health and Human Services Administration for Children and Families define sexual abstinence as "voluntarily choosing not to engage in sexual activity until marriage. Sexual activity refers to any type of genital contact or sexual stimulation between two persons including, but not limited to, sexual intercourse." This definition assures the avoidance of ALL risk associated with sexual activity.

In contrast, CSE [comprehensive sex education] programs inaccurately present an ambiguous definition of abstinence, with some stating that abstinence is "anything you want it to mean." . . .

Examples from Comprehensive Sex Education Curricula:

- "Imagine someone has decided to be **ABSTINENT**. According to your own definition of 'abstinence,' circle the following sexual behaviors you believe a person can engage in and **still be ABSTINENT**." Among the choices: 'reading erotic literature; cuddling naked; mutual masturbation; showering together; watching porn; talking sexy.'

- Abstinence may include "sexually pleasurable things without having intercourse (e.g. masturbation, kissing, talking, massaging, having fantasies, etc.)"

- "Ask participants what sexual behaviors a person **could** engage in and still be 'abstinent.'"

- "Participants will define sexual abstinence for themselves."

"What So-Called 'Comprehensive' Sex Education Teaches to America's Youth," National Abstinence Education Association, June 2007.

whelming focus of these curricula (28 percent of the curriculum content) is devoted to promoting contraception among teens.

The government already spends far more promoting contraception than it does on abstinence education. In 2002 alone, federal and state governments spent $12 on safe sex and contraception promotion programs for every $1 spent on abstinence education. Yet some members of Congress would like to eliminate even this small amount of funding that encourages teen abstinence through programs like Best Friends.

Congressional opponents of abstinence education continue to attempt to introduce legislation that would abolish federal abstinence education assistance. For example, a proposal by Sen. Max Baucus (D-MT) would take federal funds that are devoted to teaching abstinence and turn them over to state public health bureaucracies to spend as they wish. Given the fact that such bureaucracies, through the encouragement of federal funding, have been wedded to the "safe sex" approach for decades and fiercely oppose teaching abstinence, such a proposal would effectively abolish federal abstinence education programs. These funds comprise nearly all the governmental support for teaching abstinence in U.S. schools.

Opponents of abstinence education will continue to try to eliminate it from America's schools. But they have got a tough pitch to make: Parents overwhelmingly support the abstinence message. Students want to hear it. The evidence of abstinence programs' effectiveness is increasing. And the evaluation of the Best Friends program provides yet one more argument in favor of abstinence education.

"But it is also true that when everyone is forced into the pool, some people's moral or religious convictions are violated."

Employers and Insurers Should Be Able to Refuse to Cover Birth Control

Sheldon Richman

In 2004, the California Supreme Court ruled that prescription-drug plans provided by employers must cover birth control, even if the employer's religious beliefs do not include contraception. In the following viewpoint, Sheldon Richman argues that our society should not force individuals—or employers—to pay for services that they do not want, even if others do. He maintains that individuals and employers should be able to pick and choose the services they need and not have the government dictate which services should be included in their insurance policies. Richman wrote this article for The Freeman, *of which he is the editor.*

As you read, consider the following questions:

1. What kinds of state laws regarding medical services and products are cited by Sheldon Richman?

Sheldon Richman, "Freedom of Conscience and the Welfare State," *Freeman*, vol. 54, June 2004, pp. 24–26. Copyright 2004 Foundation for Economic Education, Incorporated. www.fee.org. All rights reserved. Reproduced by permission.

2. According to the author, what 1972 Wisconsin law was struck down by the Supreme Court?

3. In Richman's opinion, what is the point of the welfare state?

Who says the welfare state respects freedom of conscience? Consider: In March [2004] the California Supreme Court ruled that employer-provided prescription-drug plans must cover birth-control products, even if contraception violates an employer's religious convictions.

The conscientious objector in the case is Catholic Charities of Sacramento. The nonprofit organization, which is part of the Roman Catholic Church, argued that because Catholic doctrine condemns contraception, Catholic Charities qualifies for the exemption written into the law.

But the court saw it differently, ruling that the exemption applies only to churches, not to affiliated organizations. As the *New York Times* reported: "[T]he State Supreme Court ruled that the organization did not meet any of the criteria defining a religious employer under the law, which was passed in 1999. Under that definition, an employer must be primarily engaged in spreading religious values, employ mostly people who hold the religious beliefs of the organization, serve largely people with the same religious beliefs, and be a nonprofit religious organization as defined under the federal tax code."

Contraception Violates Catholic Teachings

The executive director of the California Catholic Conference, Ned Dolejsi, said the court does not grasp the relationship between Catholic Charities and the church. As the *Times* quoted him: "Every Catholic Charities is part of the Catholic diocese in the area where it is. Officially and formally, Catholic Charities of Sacramento is part of the Catholic Church in Sacramento, answerable to the local bishop and providing the services the church provides as a religious organization."

How comforting is it that legislatures formulate criteria for who qualifies as a religious employer, and courts decide who meets those criteria? Is Catholic Charities sufficiently part of the Catholic Church to qualify for exemption from an intrusive law? Some judges will let you know. Nineteen other states have similar mandates, and a challenge is underway in New York, brought by Catholic and Protestant plaintiffs.

This sort of thing is not supposed to happen in a free society. Yet it does, because state legislatures have become bazaars at which providers and users of medical services and products lobby to have those things incorporated by mandate into employer-provided medical plans. The politicians are happy to oblige. Besides birth control, state mandates include "treatment" for drug and alcohol use, infertility services, hair transplants and toupees, marriage and pastoral counseling, and Viagra. States have enacted more than a thousand such mandates nationwide.

Unfair to Force Insurance on Those Who Don't Want It

The motives of the parties are easily discerned. The providers anticipate more business if people don't have to pay for their products and services out of pocket. The users prefer that someone other than themselves foot the bill. Unrepresented in the lobbying frenzies are people who neither want the products and services nor want to pay for other people's use.

Insurance once meant the pooling of resources against financial ruin from possible but unlikely catastrophes. Today people expect medical insurance to cover volitional acts, such as taking birth control pills, or events that are not diseases and often are volitional, such as pregnancy. In other words, insurance has become a way to have other people pay your bills. That's one reason the health care system is such a mess. Insurance relieves us of the need to be cost-vigilant. The chief consideration is: "Does my insurance cover that?" If the answer is yes, there is no need to inquire further about necessity or price. This perverse system guarantees that demand will increase and prices for services will be bid higher than they would have been. This, in turn, makes medical insurance more expensive, discouraging more employers from offering it. (Special tax treatment rigs the system in favor of employer-based plans.)

Freedom to Choose Specific Coverage

Coercion is the key. There is nothing to stop insurance companies from offering any coverage customers want. But if insurers wish to stay in business, premiums would have to reflect the cost of the services, including administrative overhead. People who don't want coverage for contraception or alcoholism programs or hair transplants would buy basic, and cheaper, policies. Anyone who wanted that coverage would have to pay for it.

Advocates of insurance mandates point out that the per capita cost is lower when it is spread among more people. That may be true, although the stimulated demand and price rise might wipe out the savings. But it is also true that when everyone is forced into the pool, some people's moral or religious convictions are violated. Hence, Catholics pay for contraception even if they have no intention of taking advantage of the mandate. Do we really want to run roughshod over some people's consciences just so other people won't have to pay the full price for their choices?

Violation of conscience is nothing new in the welfare state. The U.S. Supreme Court has ruled that legislatures may pass laws against using a substance (such as peyote) even when it is part of religious observance. The courts have not been consistent, however. In 1972, the Supreme Court struck down a Wisconsin law that compelled parents to keep their children in school until age 16 even though the Amish conscientiously objected. Self-employed Amish are exempt from paying the

---

Requiring Contraceptive Insurance Coverage Will Lead to Coverage for Abortions

Requiring employers and insurers to cover contraceptives regardless of their moral and financial dilemmas opens the door for laws requiring employers and insurers to provide coverage for abortion. The abortion lobby will likely use the same rationalizations for contraceptive equity laws to justify mandated insurance coverage of abortion. Proponents of contraceptive equity laws believe abortion, like contraception, is a key and vital healthcare service. Supporters of contraceptive equity laws will likely claim women need abortion, just as much as they need contraception, to deal with the social and economic consequences of unplanned pregnancies. The abortion lobby used this strategy when it first sought to create a privacy right to contraception in *Griswold v. Connecticut,* and used its victory in *Griswold* to justify a right to abortion in *Roe v. Wade.*

Alex Chan, *"The Danger of 'Contraceptive Equity' Laws,"*
Americans United for Life, 2008.

Social Security payroll tax, but not so for Amish who work for others. Moreover, Amish employers are compelled to withhold the tax for their employees, despite their conviction that Social Security violates their "take care of our own" ethic. By the same token, the Amish request for exemption from child-labor laws has not been honored.

Respect the Rights of Each Individual

Even the narrow exceptions make a larger point: The state does not take seriously an individual's moral objection to compulsory "benefits." Before an exemption is considered, the authorities have to be satisfied that the objection is rooted in established religious doctrine. An individual with "merely" personal philosophical convictions against compulsion, however well-grounded in reason, has no standing. How odd for a country founded on the principles of individualism.

None of this should be surprising. The point of the welfare state is to compel universal participation. If the state required payment from only those who wanted the benefits, it would be indistinguishable from a private organization. For the system to "work," everyone must take part—whether he wants to or not. But this means that conscience cannot intrude. Occasionally, the government will yield, but only in carefully defined cases that cannot be readily broadened into a full recognition of the individual's right to personal integrity.

In other words, freedom of conscience must always take a backseat to the ambitions of social engineers.

> *"Many employers and insurance compa-*
> *nies. . .continue to refuse to cover con-*
> *traception despite legal rulings finding*
> *that failure to provide contraceptive*
> *equity is illegal sex discrimination and*
> *research showing health benefits and*
> *cost savings."*

Employers and Insurers Should Not Be Able to Refuse to Cover Birth Control

NARAL Pro-Choice America Foundation

In the following viewpoint, National Abortion Rights Action League (NARAL) Pro-Choice America Foundation argues that employers should have to include contraceptive coverage in the insurance they offer their employees. The foundation contends that coverage guarantees a woman's access to birth control, prevents unplanned pregnancies, and reduces the number of abortions. NARAL also cites studies that examine the physical and financial impacts of unintended pregnancies on women, children, and society. NARAL Pro-Choice America Foundation is an advocacy group that supports a woman's right to privacy and to choose.

NARAL Pro-Choice America Foundation, "Insurance Coverage for Contraception: A Proven Way to Protect and Promote Women's Health," *NARAL Pro-Choice America Foundation*, November 20, 2006. Reproduced by permission.

As you read, consider the following questions:

1. According to the authors, what do statistics show about children of unplanned pregnancies?
2. How many states have contraceptive-equity plans, according to this viewpoint?
3. Which legal case cited in this article was the first case in the United States to consider a federal sex discrimination claim based on the failure of an employer to cover contraception?

Access to contraception is central to women's autonomy, and equality. Contraception is basic health care and should be treated as such as a matter of public policy. The average woman will spend five years pregnant or trying to get pregnant, and nearly three decades trying to avoid pregnancy. It is estimated that without contraception she would have between 12 and 15 pregnancies. Her body and the very course of her life would be governed almost solely by reproduction. Therefore, access to contraception is critical.

Laws promoting insurance coverage for contraception are crucial to protecting and promoting women's health. By guaranteeing that insurers cover prescription contraception to the same extent as other drugs, contraceptive-equity laws help ensure women's access to birth control and ultimately prevent unintended pregnancies and reduce the need for abortion. Yet, nearly half of the states fail to guarantee contraceptive equity. Policymakers and advocates must continue to advocate for contraceptive-equity laws to help ensure women's access to this basic health-care need.

Putting Women's and Children's Health at Risk

Inadequate access to contraception carries substantial health risks for women. Not every contraceptive method is medically appropriate for every woman. Many women who use contraception rely on a reversible method that requires a prescription and, typically, a visit to a health-care provider. When all of the common methods of reversible prescription contraception are not available or affordable, some women may choose less appropriate methods or forego birth control altogether to avoid paying high, out-of-pocket costs—which may lead to unintended pregnancy.

Unintended pregnancy has serious health consequences for both woman and child. Enhanced and improved access to contraception reduces unintended pregnancy and thereby benefits both women's and children's health.

Women facing unplanned pregnancies are less likely to identify health risks associated with pregnancy prior to conception, and, therefore, often do not take full advantage of the health options available to manage such conditions safely during pregnancy.

Women facing unintended pregnancy are more likely to delay prenatal care. Studies have repeatedly shown that early and regular prenatal care is beneficial to both a woman and her pregnancy. Prenatal care allows health providers to prevent, detect, and treat problems early in a woman's pregnancy before they become serious for either the woman or baby.

Statistically speaking, children of unplanned pregnancies are at greater risk of low birth weight, dying before reaching their first birthday, of being abused, and of receiving insufficient resources in order to ensure healthy development.

Money Is Saved When Birth Control Is Covered

By preventing unintended pregnancies, insurance coverage for contraceptives also saves money.

Insurers generally pay the medical costs of unintended pregnancy, including: full-term pregnancy ($8619), ectopic pregnancy ($4994), miscarriage ($1038), and less often, abortion ($416).

Studies show that any increase in cost due to contraceptive coverage is minimal and countered by the decrease in costs associated with unintended pregnancy. According to a Guttmacher Institute study, providing coverage for the full range of reversible prescription contraceptives costs only $1.43 per employee per month—an increase of less than one percent in an employer's costs of providing medical coverage. A Washington Business Group on Health Study, which also considers the savings related to reducing unplanned pregnancies, finds that providing coverage for these methods does not ultimately increase costs.

More States Have Contraceptive-Equity Laws

Through laws, regulations, or legal opinions, 27 states now ensure that health-insurance plans that cover prescription drugs provide equitable coverage for contraceptives (AZ, AR, CA, CT, DE, GA, HI, IL, IA, ME, MD, MA, MI, MO, MT, NV, NH, NJ, NM, NY, NC, OR, RI, VT, WA, WV and WI).

As a recent study by the Guttmacher Institute reveals, passage of these state contraceptive-equity laws has dramatically improved insurance coverage for contraception, enhancing women's health and well-being. For example:

- In 1993, only 28 percent of employer-purchased insurance plans covered a full range of contraceptive methods. By 2002, that figure had almost tripled, to 86 percent. That is, almost nine in ten group health insurance plans purchased by employers for their employees now cover a full range of prescription contraceptives.

- In 1993, 28 percent of employer-purchased insurance plans covered none of the most common contraceptive methods at all. By 2002, that figure had plummeted to 2 percent.

- In states with contraceptive-equity laws, women's access to contraceptive coverage has expanded dramatically. Insurance plans in these states are more likely to provide a full range of contraceptive methods.

- State contraceptive-equity laws have a positive influence even in states lacking such laws. Nationally determined insurance plans, in use both in states with and without contraceptive-equity laws, typically provide contraceptive coverage in *all* states in accordance with the mandates.

Federal Legislation Is Needed

Despite these impressive strides toward contraceptive equity, many women still lack contraceptive coverage. For example, approximately half of all Americans that have employer-sponsored insurance coverage work for employers that opt for self-insured plans, which are regulated by the federal government and are exempt from contraceptive-equity laws and other state laws under the Employee Retirement Income Security Act (ERISA).

Given that almost two-thirds of all adult women get their health insurance through employers, continued advocacy for contraceptive-equity laws is imperative.

Refusal to Provide Coverage Is Sex Discrimination

The federal Equal Employment Opportunity Commission and federal courts have decidedly stated that refusal to provide contraceptive coverage constitutes sex discrimination and as a result, a number of companies have been required to, or have voluntarily started, offering contraceptive coverage.

Equal Employment Opportunity Commission (EEOC) Decision: In December 2000, the EEOC ruled that an employer's failure to provide coverage for contraceptive drugs, devices, and services when it covers other preventive measures constitutes sex discrimination under federal law. This ruling makes it clear that equal treatment in the workplace means women are entitled to benefits packages that include equitable coverage for prescription contraceptives.

Erickson v. Bartell Drug Co.: In 2000, pharmacist Jennifer Erickson sued her employer, Bartell Drug Co., after Bartell's health plan refused to cover her birth-control prescription even though it covered other prescription drugs. In 2001, a federal district court in Seattle, citing the EEOC decision, ruled that an employer's failure to provide coverage for prescription contraceptives in an otherwise comprehensive prescription-drug plan is sex discrimination under federal law. The *Erickson* court was the first in the country to consider a federal sex discrimination claim based on an employer's failure to provide contraceptive coverage. According to the decision, "[T]he exclusion of prescription contraceptives [from a generally comprehensive prescription plan] creates a gaping hole in the coverage offered to female employees, leaving a fundamental and immediate health care need uncovered."

Mauldin v. Wal-Mart Stores, Inc.: In October 2001, Lisa Smith Mauldin, a customer-service manager who earned approximately $12 an hour, sued her employer, Wal-Mart Stores, Inc., for excluding prescription contraceptives from its prescription-drug plan. In announcing the lawsuit, Mauldin's attorney explained, "For many women like the plaintiff, Lisa Mauldin, the $30 a month cost of birth control pills is an overwhelming financial burden and creates a barrier to obtaining quality health care." In December 2006, the Mauldin case was dismissed from federal district court in Atlanta, as a result of Wal-Mart's decision to cover prescription contraceptives in its basic employee health plan.

Dow Jones & Company Settlement: In December 2002, three Dow Jones & Co. employees successfully negotiated a settlement with the company after filing sex discrimination charges

---

Viagra Is Covered, But Not Contraceptives

[Judge Laurie Camp] Smith noted [in her ruling in a case brought against Union Pacific Railroad for its exclusion of prescription contraceptive coverage] that pregnancy brings about fatigue, nausea, vomiting, constipation, heartburn, leg cramps, sleeping problems, diabetes, and other medical conditions. Contraceptive medication prevents these problems. As a result, to treat high blood pressure medications differently from oral contraceptives is to deny only women access to a medication that prevents serious medical conditions. (Note: [Union Pacific Railroad] covers drugs for treatment of erectile dysfunction).

Leonard H. Glantz and Michael A. Grodin,
"Contraceptive Coverage Wins a Round,"
Boston Globe, *August 20, 2005.*

---

with the EEOC. The charges stemmed from the company's policy of excluding contraceptive coverage from all but one of its health plans. As a result of the settlement, all Dow Jones employees and their dependents will have insurance coverage for all FDA-approved prescription contraceptives and related medical services.

DaimlerChrysler Lawsuit: In May 2002, automaker DaimlerChrysler was sued for not including contraceptive coverage in its health insurance plan. One month after four women filed the lawsuit claiming that the DaimlerChrysler Health Care Benefits Plan's exclusion of coverage for prescription contraceptives constituted sex discrimination, DaimlerChrysler expanded its employee benefits package to include coverage for contraceptives. In March 2003, the company's request to dismiss the lawsuit was refused. The court ordered that the case be referred to alternative dispute resolution, and in March 2005, the parties reached a settlement.

EEOC v. United Parcel Services: In April 2001, a federal district court in Minnesota held that the EEOC stated a claim for intentional disparate treatment and disparate impact when it alleged that UPS's exclusion of oral contraceptives from a health benefit plan constituted sex discrimination. The court rejected United Parcel Services's claim that the exclusion was gender neutral and refused to dismiss the case.

The Public Supports Contraceptive Equity

Polls have indicated that the public not only supports equity in contraceptive coverage, but also supports legislation guaranteeing that private insurance plans include these services:

- In a 2001 NARAL Pro-Choice America Foundation nationwide poll, 77 percent of respondents supported legislation ensuring health insurance companies cover the cost of contraception.

- A 1998 Kaiser Family Foundation survey found that about three-quarters of Americans agreed with policies to guarantee that insurance plans will cover contraception—even if premiums were to rise as a result.

Employers and Companies Must Offer Coverage

Many employers and insurance companies, particularly in states without contraceptive-equity laws, continue to refuse to cover contraception despite legal rulings finding that failure to provide contraceptive equity is illegal sex discrimination and research showing health benefits and cost savings. Policy makers must continue to advocate for contraceptive-equity laws to ensure that women have access to this basic health care need. Such policies will help prevent unintended pregnancies and reduce the need for abortion and are required as a simple matter of justice and equality.

> "The best way to avoid social conflict is
> to respect everyone's conscience when-
> ever possible. That's what free choice
> should mean in a liberal democracy like
> our own."

Pharmacists Should Be Able to Refuse to Dispense Birth Control

Doug Bandow

*Doug Bandow is a senior fellow at the Cato Institute and was a
special assistant to President Ronald Reagan. In the following
viewpoint, he contends that a pharmacist should be allowed to
follow his moral and religious beliefs and refuse to fill birth control and "morning-after" pill prescriptions because a doctor is
able to refuse to perform abortions. Writing in* The American
Spectator, *Bandow argues that a woman who needs birth control could go to another pharmacy that would fill the prescription. He believes that the government should not attempt to
overrule an individual's right to follow his conscience.*

As you read, consider the following questions:

1. According to Doug Bandow, what are several of the
   most divisive political issues in this country today?

2. What does the "conscience clause" permit pharmacists and doctors and hospitals to do, according to the author?

3. In the author's opinion, what does "I opt out, but I won't stop others" mean?

Abortion, gay rights and marriage, euthanasia, and the like are among today's most contentious political issues. They tend to inflame people's worst emotions.

Choosing sides often isn't easy. For instance, no one should feel comfortable about having the state rebuff a woman's desire for an abortion, but the procedure destroys a human life. The government should not discriminate against gays, but marriage plays a unique role in providing a framework for child-rearing and family life.

The Right to Make Your Own Decisions

What should be a simple decision is allowing people to say no, irrespective of the government's stance. If abortion is legal, no doctor should have to perform it. If assisted suicide is permissible, no medical professional should have to participate.

If gay relationships are left untouched by the authorities, no apartment owner should have to rent to a same-sex couple. If contraceptives are available like other medicines, no doctor should have to write a prescription nor any pharmacist have to fill one.

In short, if "choice" is a virtue, it should be a virtue for everyone. Unfortunately, however, many liberal interest groups seem to believe that choice means allowing them to choose for everyone else.

Conscience Clauses for Pharmacists

The latest cause celebre involves pharmacists who won't fill prescriptions for birth control or the "morning after" pill. Before that it was insurers who wouldn't provide contraceptive coverage and employers who wouldn't offer marital benefits to same-sex partners.

Earlier controversies surrounded doctors and hospitals who wouldn't perform abortions. Even before that were cases of religious property owners who didn't want to rent to unmarried couples.

The political battle has been joined, with many states approving "conscience clauses" allowing doctors and hospitals to opt out of abortions and pharmacists to refuse to dispense some drugs. But Illinois Gov. Rod Blagojevich prefers coercion over conscience, and has required pharmacies to fulfill birth control prescriptions. Three states are considering legislation to do the same.

Even the supposedly freedom-loving American Civil Liberties Union (ACLU) tends to favor forcing people to set aside their moral sensitivities to provide politically correct "reproductive" services. States the ACLU: "religious objections should not be allowed to stand in the way" of care in many cases.

Whose Morality?

The real issue apparently is fear of citizens acting on their beliefs. Worries columnist Ellen Goodman, "how much further do we want to expand the reach of individual conscience?" Apparently the primary social problem today is too many people caring too much about virtue. We'd all be better off if we dropped our silly moral inhibitions.

In this view one set of moral presumptions should trump all others. Someone engaging in an activity thought to be morally wrong, or at least suspect, has a right to aid and support from others. Do whatever you want while forcing everyone else to give you whatever you want.

What if someone who desires to, say, heal others, but believes that abortion or contraception contradicts that commitment? In Goodman's view, they are asking for "conscience without consequence."

There's no real moral conflict, she suggests, since they could just quit their jobs. Which in the case of doctors and pharmacists presumably means leaving their professions. Property owners should just sell off homes in which they aren't living. And so on.

Imposing Government's Will Unfairly

If people don't follow Ms. Goodman's advice? Coerce them. Chris Taylor of the Planned Parenthood Advocates of Wisconsin demanded "a strong penalty" for pharmacist Neil Noesen who refused to fill a birth control prescription.

What is this but allowing people to ignore conscience without consequence? Protecting people from the impact of public disapproval eliminates one of the most important social tools for imparting and shaping morals.

Moreover, using government to impose a conscienceless amorality on everyone threatens a true culture war. Ms. Goodman gets it entirely wrong when she writes: "the plea to protect their conscience is a thinly veiled ploy for conquest."

A legal prohibition on abortion, or contraception, or homosexuality would be an attempt at "conquest." Simply saying "I opt out, but I won't stop others" seeks to resolve moral conflict without prohibiting or mandating conduct. It is the best strategy for promoting social harmony in a diverse and free society.

Otherwise, there is no middle ground for coexistence: whatever government decides determines everyone's behavior. Prohibiting something means penalizing those who provide the practice or product. Allowing something means penalizing those who do not offer the service or good. Everyone has an added incentive to seize power and impose their beliefs on others.

The best strategy is to leave government rule-making at a minimum, limited to important issues which only government

> # Be Fair to Pharmacists and Women
>
> Legislators at every level are attempting to settle the dispute [of whether a pharmacist should have the right to refuse filling a prescription based on moral objections]. While bills introduced at the state level have varied widely, a consensus appears to be emerging within the federal government. Both the Access to Legal Pharmaceuticals Act (S.809) and the Workplace Religious Freedom Act (S.677) were introduced in 2005, and both take the same approach: They allow a pharmacist to refuse a prescription but make sure that another pharmacist can fill it. Everyone from John Kerry, D-Massachusetts, to Rick Santorum, R-Pennsylvania, supports such legislation, but nothing has yet been passed. Until a federal bill is in place, both women and their pharmacists will remain uncertain about their rights and responsibilities.
>
> *Nate Anderson, "Pharmacists With No Plan B,"*
> Christianity Today, *August 1, 2006.*

can decide. Then, as Ms. Goodman suggests, "what holds us together is the other lowly virtue, minding your own business."

Prescriptions Can Be Filled at Different Pharmacies

Open markets even allow disagreeable people who disagree to live with a minimum of confrontation. A Chicago Planned Parenthood official argued: "A pharmacist's personal views cannot intrude on the relationship between a woman and her doctor." They don't. The woman can go elsewhere to fill a prescription.

The refusal of any one doctor, landlord, or pharmacist may be inconvenient to the customer involved. But in America today there are more than 16,000 hospitals and 51,000 retail pharmacies. Government could further increase access to contraceptives by relaxing prescription requirements.

In such a system everyone is able to choose. And everyone bears the cost of his or her choice.

A person desiring an abortion or contraceptive has to shop around. A hospital or pharmacy that refuses to offer certain services or products will lose business.

A doctor or pharmacist who won't abide by his or her employer's rules must look for another job. But life goes on, without constant legal and political battles.

Each Individual's Conscience Is Equally Important

Frances Kissling of Catholics for a Free Choice argues that "There is very little recognition that the conscience of the woman is as important, let alone more important, than the conscience of the provider." They are both important, and neither should a priori trump the other.

Are some choices simply illegitimate? Rachel Laser of the National Women's Law Center contends: refusing to fill a prescription is "outrageous. It's sex discrimination."

Actually, many of the pharmacists who say no to the abortion pill and contraceptives are women. Peggy Pace of Glen Carbon, Illinois, is one of two pharmacists suing Gov. Blagojevich over his order.

Judy Waxman of the National Women's Law Center argues that the refusal to fill prescriptions is "based on personal beliefs, not on legitimate medical or professional concerns." But the same could be said of a person desiring contraceptives or an abortion.

The belief that such products or procedures are legitimate is intrinsically no more valid than the belief that they are illegitimate. Surely the moral beliefs of medical professionals should be respected by people who emphasize the importance of "choice" and "controlling one's own body."

Keep Government Involvement to a Minimum

Unfortunately, the issue is generating widespread political war. In most states doctors have no obligation to perform an abortion. But states split over hospital provision of the procedure. A dozen states allow health professionals to refuse to offer sterilizations.

Four states authorize pharmacists to refuse to dispense contraceptives and a dozen more states are considering similar bills, while a few are threatening to go the other way. Senators Hillary Clinton (D-NY), Rick Santorum (R-PA), and John Kerry (D-MA) have introduced the Workplace Religious Freedom Act, which would offer some federal protection for dissenting pharmacists.

Few agree on all of these issues: I oppose abortion but see no moral objection to contraception or sterilization. Some people support or oppose all three. Government should leave employers, employees, and consumers free to sort out who provides what service to whom.

Public officials should remember the virtues of neutrality. The best way to avoid social conflict is to respect everyone's conscience whenever possible. That's what free choice should mean in a liberal democracy like our own.

Periodical Bibliography

The following articles have been selected to supplement the diverse views presented in this chapter.

Donna Brazile	"The Wrong Prescription," *Ms. Magazine*, Summer 2006.
Heidi Bruggink	"Miseducation: The Lowdown on Abstinence-Only Sex-Ed Programs," *The Humanist*, January-February 2007.
Alex Chan	"The Danger of 'Contraceptive Equity' Laws," Defending Life 2008, 2008. www.aul.org.
Steve Chapman	"Right to Choose v. Power to Compel," *Chicago Tribune*, April 7, 2005.
Michelle Chen	"Teaching Kids About Sex," *Gotham Gazette*, October 25, 2007. www.gothamgazette.com.
Rebekah E. Gee	"Plan B, Reproductive Rights, and Physician Activism," *The New England Journal of Medicine*, July 6, 2006.
Jaana Goodrich	"The Conscience Clause," *The American Prospect*, April 2006.
Mark Malouse	"Pharmacists Must Exercise Conscience," *Times-Picayune*, May 14, 2005.
Ruth Marcus	"Daughter Knows Best," *The Washington Post*, October 24, 2007.
National Women's Law Center	"Contraceptive Coverage: A Multi-Track Approach," National Women's Law Center, September 2007. www.nwlc.org.
Robert Rector	"Aborting Abstinence," *National Review*, April 29, 2005. www.nationalreview.com.
Paul M. Weyrich	"Abstinence Education Programs: Changing Attitudes," Accuracy in Media, September 28, 2005. www.aim.org.

CHAPTER 3

Should Teens Have Access to Birth Control?

Chapter Preface

Almost half of all high-school students have had sex, and about 34 percent of high-school students are sexually active, according to the *2005 Youth Risk Behavior Surveillance* report from the U.S. Centers for Disease Control and Prevention (CDC). The study also found that a condom wasn't used during the last sexual experience by 34 percent of sexually active high-school students. Approximately one-third of the 750,000 pregnancies of fifteen- to nineteen-year-old women in the United States end in abortion.

As with the debate over allowing teens access to birth control, emergency contraception (EC), or Plan B, has been presented as a way to help reduce the number of abortions. If taken within seventy-two hours of unprotected sex, the drug can prevent pregnancy. On August 24, 2006, the U.S. Food and Drug Administration (FDA) approved EC to be sold over the counter (OTC) without a prescription to women eighteen years old and older. However, women seventeen years old and younger still need a prescription from their doctor.

Those who believe that teens should be allowed to buy EC without a prescription contend that it is necessary because of the negative consequences of a teenage pregnancy. In the *Albany Times Union* on September 19, 2005, Ellen Goodman wrote, "If teenagers also need Plan B, it's because Plan A, abstinence, fails more often than condoms. Too many teenagers end up pregnant, facing Plan C: abortion or motherhood. In the name of protection, we are leaving teenagers far too vulnerable."

Advocates of abstinence contend that EC should not be available to anyone, including teens, without a legal prescription because of fears that it will lead to promiscuity and concerns about health risks. Janice Shaw Crouse of Concerned Women for America writes, "Those advocating OTC availability are touting the drug as a 'silver bullet' for birth control. Yet, the easy availability that would come with OTC sales extends to those who are incapable of understanding the risks involved in any high-potency drug. Highly vulnerable potential users would include young teens as well as those of limited intelligence or education who might not understand the dangers of using Plan B routinely."

Choosing to have sex is a part of life for many teenagers, and that decision is one that advocates of abstinence and sex education continue to argue about. In the following chapter, commentators offer their opinions on the virtues and problems of teaching sex education and abstinence and whether teens should be able to obtain birth control.

| "'Our silence is becoming deadly,' she told the audience. 'Just saying no is not enough.'"

Teens Should Have Access to Birth Control

Tuala Williams

In the following viewpoint, which was published in Greater Diversity News, *Tuala Williams spoke to Joycelyn Elders, who served as the U.S. Surgeon General for President Bill Clinton during part of his first term. Elders was fired for suggesting that teachers discuss masturbation as a form of safe sex and that schools distribute condoms. Elders contends that many Americans are reluctant to talk honestly about sex and the need for condoms, which has led to the spread of HIV/AIDS, especially among African Americans. Williams is a reporter for* The Dallas Examiner.

As you read, consider the following questions:

1. According to Tuala Williams, what two other issues did Joycelyn Elders support?

2. What percentage of reported AIDS cases in 2003 happened as a result of injection drug use and/or sex with an injection drug user?

Tuala Williams, "Jocelyn Elders: Our Silence is Becoming Deadly," in *The Dallas Examiner*, December 6, 2007. Reproduced by permission of Tuala Williams.

3. According to Elders, what percentage of the people diagnosed with HIV/AIDS in 2006 were African American?

D r. M. Joycelyn Elders shocked America following her 1993 appointment as the first Black surgeon general to the United States.

Appointed by then Pres. Bill Clinton, she was embraced throughout the country for her fresh perspective on health, medicine and feminine equality, not to mention her impressive resume.

Her progression to surgeon general seemed natural, but like Bill and Hillary Clinton, her biggest fans, she was not afraid of controversy. She raised the ire of conservative Americans with widely published and televised statements about abortion, sexuality and drugs—all controversial issues in the 90s.

Encourage the Use of Birth Control

At a 1992 Arkansas state rally, Elders was quoted as saying, "We would like for the right-to-life, anti-choice groups to really get over their love affair with the fetus and start supporting the children." Promoting birth control, which included government funded condoms and abortions, Elders stated she was more concerned with quality of life than she was in bringing children into a life of poverty, lacking medical care, and facing neglect and abuse. Ironically, Elders, who grew up in poverty, without even the luxury of running water, admits to not having seen a doctor herself until she attended medical school. During her term, she also argued for the legalization of drugs and was an advocate for gay rights.

But the last straw for the American public was oddly over an issue that might barely raise an eyebrow today. The issue was that of masturbation. During a World AIDS Day event at the United Nations, December 1994, Elders was asked if she would consider promoting masturbation. According to the *US*

News & World Report, Elders responded by saying, "masturbation . . . is something that is a part of human sexuality and a part of something that should perhaps be taught."

Apparently, America wasn't ready for Elders and the backlash from the statement moved the previously supportive Clinton to request her resignation in 1994, after only 15 months in office. She was allegedly fired for, "values contrary to the administration." Ironically, Clinton would later be impeached by the House of Representatives for perjury and obstruction of justice charges related to his sexual misconduct with Monica Lewinsky.

But the question remains, was Elders totally off-base or was she merely ahead of her time? Would Elders' recommendation about promoting condoms and teaching masturbation in public schools have stemmed the tide of this growing disease?

Could Sex Ed and Birth Control Help Reduce HIV/AIDS?

While researchers have made great strides in the detection and treatment of HIV/AIDS, it remains a pandemic. Today, according to a report by the Kaiser Family Foundation, there are 1.2 million people living with HIV/AIDS in America. And as of Dec. 31, 2005, there were reported to be 13,472 persons living with HIV/AIDS in the Dallas Metroplex, as reported by the U.S. Department of HUD [Housing and Urban Development].

Could greater sexual education have helped to reduce those numbers for what is known to be a preventable, primarily sexual disease? While AIDS can be transmitted through intravenous drug use, it remains primarily a sexual disease. In fact, according to the Centers for Disease Control and Prevention, only 23 percent of new AIDS cases reported in 2003 were attributed to injection drug use and/or sex with an injection drug user.

Elders spoke out recently at a Dallas World AIDS Day luncheon hosted by AIDS Arms and nine other Ryan White funded AIDS organizations. The unprecedented collaboration was successful in drawing over 500 attendees to the event, held at the Hilton-Anatole Hotel. Prior to the luncheon, guests were allowed to visit the exhibit where the famous quilt dedicated to those who have lost their lives to AIDS was displayed. It is the largest ongoing community arts project in the world. In the U. S., over 550,394 people died from AIDS related complications during the period of 2001–2005.

No doubt, the large attendance was, in part, due to the presence of the still outspoken and controversial Elders, who has remained an advocate for the prevention and intervention of HIV/AIDS. Despite her termination as surgeon general, she continues to stand by her earlier statements, repeating many of her views during the luncheon and receiving a standing ovation following her speech.

She said the most important thing she wanted attendees to take with them was that HIV/AIDS is a disease that is still with us. There is no cure and it does not discriminate. She said 51 percent of the new diagnoses last year [2006] were people who looked like her, emphasizing that the faces of the disease have changed since the days when it was considered a largely gay-White male disease.

Educate Kids About Sex and Contraception

Citing statistics of those suffering with the disease who do not have appropriate medical care, Elders said America has "absolutely the best sick care system in the world, but no health care system."

Stating that America has a sexually unhealthy society, Elders emphasized the fact that humans are sexual beings, yet, she said we don't talk about sex enough. "We walk around and we say, well, ignorance is bliss and we misinterpret ignorance for innocence. We've got to start educating our children," she said, introducing her "ABC" list for sexual education.

"A—abstinence; B—be faithful; C—latex condoms, D—do other things, i.e., masturbation."

Elders, during her term as surgeon general, advocated the distribution of condoms in public schools. In response to the argument that condoms break, Elders responds, "Vows of abstinence break far more often than latex condoms."

Elders still suggests that masturbation be taught in schools as part of their sexual education, the goal being to prevent teenage pregnancy and the spread of sexually transmitted diseases, including HIV/AIDS. Masturbation, Elders says, is normal and healthy, "80-plus percent of women and 90 percent of men masturbate and the rest lie," she told the audience at the luncheon. In light of the HIV/AIDS scare sweeping America, she advocates self-stimulation as the safest form of sex, guaranteed to prevent infection.

Kids Having Sex at a Young Age

According to CDC's 2003 Youth Risk Behavioral Survey, "47 percent of high school students have had sexual intercourse, and 7.4 percent of them reported first sexual intercourse before age 13." An estimated 4,883 young people received a diagnosis of HIV infection or AIDS in 2004, representing about 13 percent of the persons diagnosed that year, according to a report by the Centers for Disease Control and Prevention. African-American youth are disproportionately affected by HIV infection, accounting for 55 percent of all HIV infections reported among persons aged 13–24 in 2004, the CDC stated.

She encouraged everyone to take responsibility to stop the spread of HIV/AIDS, saying that everyone can do something. "It may be reading to somebody, it may be taking them a meal or offering them a warm blanket or getting up and speaking out during difficult times. But whatever you do, make sure you do your share."

Calling for leadership and awareness in our communities, she said we must educate our schools to educate our youth, adding that parents and doctors must also be educated about sex.

Emphasizing the need for churches to do their part in addressing the disease, she said, "We certainly [need to] educate, motivate and involve our churches. We can't allow them to continue moralizing from the pulpit and preaching to the choir." Her comment was followed by thunderous applause. The church has often been accused of failing to effectively address the disease or issues related to sex among the populations they serve.

"Our silence is becoming deadly," she told the audience. "Just saying no is not enough."

> "The non-abstinent students were more likely to earn low grades, drop out of high school and experiment with drug and alcohol use."

Teens Should Not Have Access to Birth Control

Janice Shaw Crouse

Janice Shaw Crouse, who wrote this article for Townhall.com, is a Senior Fellow at the Beverly LaHaye Institute, which is the Concerned Women for America's think tank. In the following viewpoint, she contends that abstinence is more effective than comprehensive sex education in helping to reduce the number of teens having sex, teen pregnancies, and abortions. Shaw Crouse argues that sex education proponents unfairly twist evidence to try to show that abstinence doesn't work. She refers to data that show that abstinent teens are more likely to do well in school, finish high school, and avoid using alcohol or drugs.

As you read, consider the following questions:

1. According to Janice Shaw Crouse, why was Mathematica's study of abstinence programs flawed?

Janice Shaw Crouse, "Why the Left Is Attacking Abstinence Programs," Townhall.com, May 1, 2007. Reproduced by permission of the author.

2. What was the change in sexual activity among black teenagers from 1991 to 2005, according to the Centers for Disease Control?

3. What kind of comparison does the author make between the number of unwed teens having babies and the number of unmarried women giving birth?

It happens all the time—when Congress begins drafting appropriations bills dealing with the funding of sex education, the left starts undermining abstinence programs. The federal government disproportionately supports those sex education programs prominently featuring condom distribution from Planned Parenthood and other organizations that argue: "Teens are going to have sex anyway, so the best response is to teach teens to protect themselves and encourage them to practice 'safe' sex." In fact, for every $12 spent on condom-based programs, only $1 is spent funding abstinence programs. Yet when appropriations hearings are held, you can count on well-timed research being released to "prove" that the few and relatively new abstinence programs don't work. The left vehemently argues that the government is throwing money away to support abstinence programs. Translation: All the federal money should go to the groups promoting "safe sex" through the use of condoms.

Using Flawed Data to Criticize Abstinence

Often, the attacks are extreme and partisan. For instance, this weekend, the media, including the *Washington Post*, gave considerable attention to a 20-page document from The American Civil Liberties Union (ACLU), Advocates for Youth, and the Sexuality Information and Education Council of the United States (SIECUS) that simply regurgitated previous attacks on three abstinence programs. The letter criticized statistics from a 1993 program, and attacked a program no longer published and one that has been updated and revised. Obviously, such unfounded criticism puts a political agenda before honest evaluation—never mind students' well-being.

Last week, Mathematica Policy Research Inc. released a study of abstinence programs that was widely disseminated even though it was a very limited study—only four early abstinence programs—and was based on flawed methodology. The targeted children were in abstinence programs at age 9–11 and had no follow-up before being evaluated when they were 15–16 years of age.

The misleading Mathematica study made headlines in all media. An alarmist MSNBC report was headlined, "Blind faith on sex-ed approach puts kids at risk." The politically-motivated subheading declared, "Bullheaded Bush administration puts abstinence ideology before lives." The *Christian Science Monitor* put a positive headline on a very negative article. The headline: "Honesty about abstinence-only: To confront the apparent failures of these programs is not to give up on teen abstinence as a standard." In spite of the headline, however, the article used 13 paragraphs to explain how abstinence programs have produced "zero effect. That's right: zero."

Abstinence Programs Have Made a Difference

Common sense tells you that you're not likely to find something that you're determined not to see. One study of a D.C.-area program found that girls in the abstinence program were seven times less likely to engage in sexual activity than those who were not in the program. Common sense also says that something has been at work to bring down the rates of sexual activity by teens over the last 15 years. That "something at work" certainly isn't the liberal sex education bilge that has polluted the minds of teens for the last 40–50 years; the "sex is no big deal" and "sex-without-consequences" agendas of such "education" programs are hard to distinguish from the ones pushed by Hugh Hefner at Playboy. Those agendas produced unprecedented rates of teen sexual activity, out-of-wedlock births and abortions.

Yet, frequently truth breaks through the darkness of lies and distortion. Truth can even spotlight the fallacies in special-interest agendas.

For instance, the *Journal of Research on Adolescence* just published the results of a survey covering 1,052 inner-city adolescents. A team of pediatricians at New York City's Albert Einstein College of Medicine conducted the research and found that abstinent students have a stronger academic profile, while those who engage in sexual experimentation are more likely to exhibit academic and behavioral pathologies. The non-abstinent students were more likely to earn low grades, drop out of high school and experiment with drug and alcohol use. The Einstein scholars identified the "co-occurrence of substance abuse and dropping out of school with sexual activity" as a "problem behavior syndrome."

Abstinence programs don't as yet have a long track record; they've only been in place a few years, and only recently have they seen widespread use in schools across the nation. There aren't that many evaluations of the programs available, though 12 studies indicate remarkable effectiveness.

The big story, however, is the trends revealed in the official data indicating dramatic and remarkable demographic changes that coincide with the broader use of abstinence-only programs across the nation. Official government statistics show reversals in trend lines that were resistant to change prior to the availability of abstinence-only programs. These data are available, but hardly anyone is paying attention; certainly, the following three trends aren't making the headlines—and they should.

Teens Are Having Less Sex

The Centers for Disease Control reports that teen sexual activity has decreased; the downturn is especially dramatic among

Abstinence Programs Produce Results

Plenty of reliable studies demonstrate that abstinence education *does* work. . . . One study, published in the journal *Adolescent and Family Health* and based on data from National Vital Statistics Records, the National Survey of Family Growth and the Alan Guttmacher Institute (formerly the research arm of Planned Parenthood and no friend of abstinence education), notes that:

The factors most strongly related to the decline in teen pregnancies and teen births from 1991 to 1995 were an increase in abstinence and a decline in the percentage of teens who were married. Increased abstinence among teens accounted for most of the reduction in births and for 67 percent of the reduction in out-of-wedlock teenage pregnancies.

Rebecca Hagelin, "Combating the Condom Crowd," *WorldNetDaily*, January 24, 2008, www.worldnetdaily.com.

black teens—dropping from 81.4 percent in 1991 to 67.6 percent in 2005. Among Hispanics, the drop is relatively small but in the right direction—from 53.1 to 51.0. Among whites, the reversal of the trend is important because the number has stayed below 50 percent since the mid-90s and now is at 43.0 percent.

The downward trends in three population groups represent documented changes in teen behavior—even with a slight blip upward in the early 2000s, rates are still well below that of the early 1990s.

Why would we go back to programs that encourage students to engage in behavior that we know is risky—behaviors that the Einstein pediatricians indicate produce "problem behavior syndrome"?

Fewer Teens Are Having Babies

Between 1940 and 1954, the unwed birthrate for teens (15–19 years old) doubled; it doubled again by 1984, and increased another 50 percent before peaking in 1994. Since 1994, however—and in defiance of everyone's expectations—unwed teen birthrates have steadily followed a downward trend. The National Vital Statistics Report reveals that (based on preliminary data for 2005), teen birthrates are down by 25 percent since 1994.

The unwed birthrate for younger teens (15–17) declined by 12 per thousand since 1994, while the rate for older teens (18–19) declined by 11 per thousand. The older teen drop is particularly significant because from 1974–1994 their unwed birthrate paralleled the rate for unmarried early 20s women. After 1994, though, the older teen rate dropped while that of the unmarried early 20s continued to climb (though at a slower rate than in the 1980s).

It is worth repeating that this reversal of trend in the unwed teen birthrate stands in sharp contrast to the fact that the unwed birthrate for women in their 20s has continued to go up—for unmarried women 20–24, a 5 percent increase from 1994 to 2005 and among unmarried women 25–29, an astounding 25 percent increase!

The drop in teen births is particularly encouraging in that it has occurred among both black and white teens and both younger and older teens, most especially among the younger 15–17 year-old teens who have not had a chance to complete their high school education.

The rate for black teens peaked in 1991 (for 15–17 year olds: 80 per thousand in 1991 to 37 per thousand in 2004 and for 18–19 year olds a drop of nearly one-third: 149 per thousand in 1991 to 101 per thousand in 2004).

The birth rate among unmarried black teens in both age groups was lower in 2004 than it has been in over four decades.

While birth rates among unmarried black teens remain high compared to rates for unmarried white teens, the gap between black and white teens narrowed considerably during the 1990s.

For white teens the peak in unwed births was in 1994. In the post-WWII era, the birth rates among unmarried white teens in both age groups rose steadily until 1994 (from 3 per thousand to 24 among 15–17 year olds and from 8 per thousand to 56 among 18–19 year olds).

The effect of these declines in birthrates has been dramatic and is an under-reported success story about young African-American women; perhaps what has been happening among black teens can best be appreciated by translating it into the number of teen births averted. Total births to black teens declined from 136,000 in 1996 to 107,000 in 2005, a decrease of more than 21.5 percent. More than 90 percent of this decline was accounted for by the decrease in unwed teen births.

Number of Teen Abortions Has Been Cut in Half

The National Center for Health Statistics reports that the rate of teen abortions has been cut in half since 1988. At its peak, teen abortions were at 44 per 1000. Now at a dramatic low, the number is 22 per 1000. Obviously, we cannot credit today's declining teen birthrate to teens turning to abortion.

Interestingly, as teens become more abstinent, there are fewer abortions, too. One has to ask if a greater appreciation for life is a byproduct of the self-discipline and self-esteem that is required for a teen to remain abstinent.

Let's do the math. Three out of three's not bad! Especially considering that liberal researchers can't seem to find any effect from abstinence programs. During the 30-year reign of condom-based sex education, teen sexual activity increased, teen births dramatically increased and teen abortions were going up. What's different now? Have teens suddenly learned how to use condoms more effectively and consistently than adult women who are using contraception but are frequently surprised nonetheless to find themselves pregnant? Somehow, I doubt it!

Clearly, many teens have heard the truth and are abstaining from sex—a decision that is best for them in every way. Along with decreased sexual activity among teens, we are seeing corresponding decreases in teen births and teen abortions. These simultaneous reverses in trends indicate that teens are choosing a path that is proven to lead to a bright and promising future both in their personal lives and in every other aspect of their well-being.

| "The practice of sexual abstinence for youth is the best form of prevention against HIV infection, other STDs, and out-of-wedlock pregnancies."

Abstinence-Only Sex Education Should Be Taught in Schools

Moira Gaul

In the following viewpoint, Moira Gaul argues that proposed changes to health standards for District of Columbia students in grades six through nine should be revised to stress the importance of abstinence. She is critical of a curriculum that she believes puts too much emphasis on contraception, as well as sexual orientation and identity. Citing studies, Gaul maintains that encouraging children to remain abstinent works to help students to avoid other dangerous behavior, including drug use. Gaul is the director of women's and reproductive health at the Family Research Council.

As you read, consider the following questions:

1. According to Moira Gaul, what kind of negative behavior can be caused by premarital teenage sex?

Moira Gaul, "Testimony on D.C. Public Schools Sex Education," *Family Research Council*, December 21, 2007. Reproduced by permission of Family Research Council, 801 G Street, NW, Washington, DC 20001, 1-800-225-4008, www.frc.org.

2. In the 2007 Zogby poll, what percentage of parents believe that sex education classes should emphasize abstinence more than contraceptives?

3. What do studies cited by the author report about the effects of abortion on teenagers?

My name is Moira Gaul and I am the director for women's and reproductive health at the Family Research Council here in Washington, D.C. The Family Research Council is a pro-family public policy organization involved on the federal, state, and local levels. I have a masters in public health degree, with an emphasis in maternal and child health, and I work in policy areas to promote optimal healthy outcomes for women and children, as well as to strengthen families. In addition, I have also worked for three years with District youth in several faith-based programs.

The Family Research Council opposes the proposed D.C. public schools health standards [the draft of "Health Learning Standards" proposed for all students] in their current form. There are five specific standards we have identified as particularly problematic. These five standards are listed at the conclusion of this letter.

Within the overall standards, values are introduced that are not acceptable to many parents of children being served in the District of Columbia. For example, the promotion of contraception to 7th grade students, and the discussion of sexual orientation and gender identity beginning in 6th grade are completely unacceptable to many District parents. These standards do not adequately reflect the values of parents and families that the D.C. school system serves.

The proposed standards lack an approach in sexuality education that seeks the best health outcomes for our youth by encouraging them to abstain from sexual activity outside of marriage.

Pre-marital adolescent sex has been associated with a number of negative behavioral outcomes including: poor academic performance, substance abuse, mental health problems and illness, as well as increased risk for sexually transmitted diseases (STDs) and out-of-wedlock child bearing. Pre-marital adolescent sex, heterosexual or homosexual, is by definition, high-risk behavior. The practice of sexual abstinence for youth is the best form of prevention against HIV infection, other STDs, and out-of-wedlock pregnancies.

Abstinence education provides youth with the right skills necessary to successfully practice the behavior. Based on sound behavior change theory, abstinence-focused education provides youth with the skills necessary to avoid sexual activity, build character, and develop healthy relationships. It promotes optimal physical and psycho-social health in youth. Contraception focused education is a simplistic risk reduction strategy with a "physical health only" approach. The abstinence education approach, in contrast, is a multidimensional, holistic health, risk avoidance form of prevention which addresses mental, emotional, and physical health. D.C. youth deserve this support to make the best choice for their current health, future health, and future reproductive health.

We would urge the School Board to review a 2004 study by the Heritage Foundation, "Comprehensive Sex Education vs. Authentic Abstinence: A Study of Competing Curricula." In this study, content or quantitative analysis was performed on nine major comprehensive sex education/"abstinence plus" curricula and nine major authentic abstinence programs. The results showed that authentic abstinence programs devoted 53 percent of page content to abstinence-related material, and 17 percent to subjects of healthy relationships and marriage. In contrast, the comprehensive curricula devoted 4.7 percent of page content to abstinence, and zero percent to healthy relationships and marriage.

Teens Respond to the Idea of Abstinence

Where the message of abstinence is delivered, many teens are surprisingly relieved. Julie Laipply, a national speaker on successful choices, arrived at a high school to speak about abstinence. The principal said, "Have you talked to our students? Everybody has sex. They won't like your presentation. You might want to cut down your talk from 60 minutes to 15."

She didn't take him up on that request, but she did invite him to stay and watch. She took her 60 minutes and she told the students, "I'm not here to tell you what to do, but I want to share some information and remind you that you do have a choice." She spoke of the physical and emotional consequences of teens having sex, and at the end of her presentation, the students spontaneously applauded. They sensed that her message was about their long-term health and well-being and they did not have to succumb to peer pressure.

Maurine Jensen Proctor, "Abstinence Under Fire,"
Meridian Magazine, *2007.*

Additionally, this risk avoidance or abstinence approach is mutually reinforcing across youth high-risk behaviors (concerning alcohol, tobacco, and drug use, and violence). Currently in the health standards a uniform risk avoidance message is emphasized to youth concerning alcohol, tobacco and drug use, and violence. The science shows adolescent risk behaviors are so interconnected that to be effective in guiding youth away from one major risk behavior, all major risk behaviors, including sexual risk taking, must be addressed.

Parents also prefer abstinence until marriage as the best form of prevention for their children. A recent 2007 Zogby poll showed that 83 percent of parents think it is important for their child to wait until they are married to have sex; 78 percent of parents think sex education classes in public schools should place more emphasis on promoting abstinence than on condom and other contraceptive use; and 93 percent of parents agree sex education should include a discussion about the limitations of condoms in preventing specific STDs.

One example of intensive, successful abstinence-focused programming is Best Friends in Washington, D.C. An independent study of this program was published in the peer-reviewed journal *Adolescent and Family Health* in 2005. The young women who participate in the program are called "Diamond Girls," and they hail from some of the District's toughest wards. Study author Robert Lerner, Ph.D., found that the Diamond Girls "are substantially less likely to smoke, drink, take illegal drugs, and have sex than a comparable sample" of youth in the Centers for Disease Control and Prevention's surveys. The finding of the study that Diamond Girls are 120 times more likely to abstain from sex than their peers "is a result so strong that it is unheard of in practically any empirical research." Programs like Best Friends are succeeding because they aim high and sell no one short.

We are also strongly opposed to the promotion of abortion to 9th graders as specified in the draft standards. The abortion rate for school-aged girls in the District of Columbia is one of the highest in the nation. The D.C. public schools should not be lending support to the perpetuation of this destructive trend which harms girls' and women's health. Studies analyzing the effects of induced abortion in adolescents have shown that, when compared to adolescents who give birth, those who abort reported more frequent problems sleeping, more frequent marijuana use, and increased need for psychological counseling.

In addition, the standards need to emphasize healthy family formation, including a two-parent family where the marriage of one man and one woman is promoted as the best parenting structure for children, and where the best outcomes for children have been established repeatedly in the social science research. Healthy marriage components need to be introduced to students also to aid in the building of strong future families.

Lastly, we would recommend that interventions include parental components to increase overall impact.

"As the schools relinquish responsibility for educating American teens about sex, the advertisers and networks step in, providing an airbrushed, inauthentic, unrealistic view of sex and the bodies that are 'doing it.'"

Abstinence-Only Sex Education Should Not Be Taught in Schools

Courtney E. Martin

Courtney E. Martin, who wrote this article for Alternet.org, is the author of Perfect Girls, Starving Daughters: The Frightening New Normalcy of Hating Your Body. *In the following viewpoint, she argues that teaching children only about abstinence doesn't fully prepare them to deal with the conflicting body images and stereotypes that society and the media offer. Martin contends that knowledge about contraceptives and sex allows teens to make more informed decisions about their bodies. She maintains that the conflicting views offered by society about the roles of men and women confuse teenagers.*

As you read, consider the following questions:

1. In Courtney Martin's opinion, in what dual roles does society place boys?

2. According to the author, how many children have had sex by the time they're 15 after having been taught abstinence-only sex education?

3. What kind of connection is there between eating disorders and victims of sexual assault, according to Martin?

As the middle-aged gym teacher in a track suit stands in front of the class and reads a health book out loud in a monotone voice—"Intercourse can lead to unwanted pregnancy and sexually transmitted diseases, such as . . ."—a couple of girls swap the latest issue of *US Weekly* and a *Gossip Girls* novel, all the juicy parts underlined in pink pen. Welcome to contemporary American adolescence, where sexuality is either up for sale or moralized into nonexistence.

On the one hand we have a hypersexualized and pornified pop culture—thongs marketed to tweens, Victoria's Secret ads with models who don't look a day over 13, and reality shows like *A Shot at Love* on MTV, where both men and women will do anything—including jump in vats of chocolate and discuss their sexual histories on national television—all for instantaneous love with a petite model. The message to young women is loud and clear: Your body is your power. Flaunt it. Use it. Get attention. The message to young men is also unmistakable: Your gaze is your power. Your role is to judge and comment on women's bodies. As a man, you are inevitably obsessed—sometimes stupidly so—with the female form.

Telling Kids That Abstinence Will Solve All Problems

On the other hand, we have a federally funded (over $1 billion thus far) abstinence-only sex education program in this country. According to the Guttmacher Institute, nearly half

(46 percent) of all 15- to 19-year-olds in the United States have had sex at least once. According to the government's most comprehensive survey of American sexual practices to date, more than half of all teenagers have engaged in oral sex—including nearly a quarter of those who have never had intercourse. Regardless of this reality, health teachers from Nacogdoches, Texas, to Newark, N.J., are taught to emotionlessly repeat—as if pull dolls of the Bush administration—"The only guaranteed way to avoid pregnancy and STDs is abstinence. The only guaranteed way to avoid pregnancy and STDs is abstinence. The only guaranteed way to avoid pregnancy and STDs is abstinence."

Here, the message to young women is also resolute: Your body is dangerous. Control it. Ignore it. Don't ask any questions. Teen girls are cast as asexual princesses happily trapped in towers, guarded by their Bible verse-spouting fathers. The message to young men is more subtle. In this fairy tale written, produced and directed by abstinence-only advocates, teenage guys are both potential villains—the oversexed, hormone-crazed young men who must be refused continuously by good girls—or potential knights in shining armor—saving enough money from their summer jobs to buy sparkling rings that will save their sweeties from the hell of slutdom.

In between pornified culture and purity balls, in between the slut and the virgin, the stupid, lascivious dude and the knight in shining armor, in between the messages directed at young women—your body is your power vs. your body is dangerous—and young men—your gaze is your power vs. your gaze is dangerous—are real young people trying to develop authentic identities and sexual practices. And they are struggling mightily.

Too many of them are diseased, disordered, and depressed—participating in inauthentic performances of sexual bravado, cut off from their bodies' true appetites and desires, and hurt because they can't seem to identify or communicate their own boundaries.

Not Preparing Teens for the Real World

How could we be surprised? We've constructed a polarized culture that gives teenagers edifice, not education. We've sent them out into the wildly complex country of contemporary adolescence without the essential weapons—sexual literacy, communication strategies, self-reflection exercises, and at the very least, accurate information about anatomy and contraception.

We've let the increasingly conglomerated raunchy mass media pollute the visual world with plastic, codified images of "sex" and the increasingly out-of-touch, religious and righteous federal government play Pollyanna—deaf, dumb and blind. As the schools relinquish responsibility for educating American teens about sex, the advertisers and networks step in, providing an airbrushed, inauthentic, unrealistic view of sex and the bodies that are "doing it." They're happy to play sexy nanny while our government officials and educators are out to lunch; it guarantees ratings and the next generation eager to fork over cash on products marketed to their effectively socialized inadequacy.

And what kind of education do we provide to help negotiate this onslaught of messages? A curriculum based on three little empty words: "Just say no." Even federally funded studies of abstinence-only sex education confirm that it is ineffective. Half of those who have abstinence-only sex ed end up having sex by the time they're 15 years old. Multiple peer-reviewed studies also confirm that purity pledges actually lead teenagers into having more oral, anal and unprotected sex. Another longitudinal study of 13,000 teenagers found that 53 percent of those who commit to purity until marriage have sex out of wedlock within the year.

Treat Teens with Respect

Teenagers don't like to feel like they're being treated as children. We don't like to think we're not being told the whole story just because of our age. After years of being taught basic concepts, only to be told that what we were first taught is in fact an oversimplification and mostly wrong, many students become belligerent about not being told the whole story.

Joel Minor, "Straight Talk at School,"
Denver Post, April 15, 2007.

Women Are Suffering Because of Abstinence-Only Education

The consequences are devastating, diverse and rampant. According to the Rape, Abuse, and Incest National Network, every two and a half minutes, somewhere in America, someone is sexually assaulted. About 44 percent of rape victims are under age 18, and 80 percent are under age 30. According to the Guttmacher Institute, of the 18.9 million new cases of STDs each year, 9.1 million (48 percent) occur among 15- to 24-year-olds. Seven million girls and women in this country have eating disorders; clinicians estimate that as many as 80 percent of those with anorexia, bulimia and binge-eating disorder are victims of sexual assault.

And harder to pin down with numbers, most college (and some high school) students experience campuses characterized by random, unsatisfying hookups, stunted emotional growth and the private hell of loneliness, guilt and shame. So many young adults don't know how to deal with the messiness of sex without being sloppy drunk.

We could make such a difference by doing so little. First and foremost, we must replace abstinence-only sexual education with comprehensive curriculum that teaches teenagers accurate, useful and wide-ranging information. They are welcome to save intercourse for marriage, of course, and should certainly be taught that—indeed—it is one of only two ways to absolutely prevent pregnancy, though not STDs. (The method of sexual exploration that guarantees both no STDs and no pregnancy is, of course, masturbation!) But they must also be given the tools—informational, emotional, communicative—they need should they choose otherwise. We need to teach both young women and men about sexual desire—that it varies widely and is not shameful but can be overwhelming.

We must also provide our kids with the media and consumer literacy needed to face the pornified culture that we live in and advocate—through letter writing, boycotts, and public pressure—that schools, playgrounds, and other public spaces remain advertising-free. As artists, filmmakers, writers, actors, producers etc., we must strive to provide a more enlightened and inspiring view of human sexuality, to create work that involves love and sex without codifying both into unreality. Think Jane Campion.

Teens Are Capable of Understanding the Facts of Life

And finally, we must stop treating teenagers as if they are either dangerous or idiots. When I was recently on *The O'Reilly Factor* with conservative pundit Laura Ingraham, she shouted, in response to my apparently blasphemous idea that girls deserve to be educated about their bodies: "Twelve-year-olds can't even pick out what color shirt they want to wear in the morning!" It made me wonder if Laura had ever met a 12-year-old, ever had a real conversation with one about her dreams, her thoughts, her desires.

I've had the pleasure of interacting with many teenagers—12 years old and older—and I'm continually amazed at their insight, maturity and earnest need for more information. They aren't adults yet—sure—but they are aching in that direction. They need those of us who are done with the journey to provide some fundamental tools on how to make it through. We need to ask them about what they're experiencing and how we can be helpful as they make their way. Instead of luring them in, selling them out, condemning or indoctrinating them, we need to meet them face to face with compassion and information.

> *"A culture that bans tanning, but gives the green light for contraception and abortion for school-age girls has indeed lost sight of what is important."*

Teenagers Should Need Their Parents' Permission to Obtain Birth Control

Father John Flynn

In the following viewpoint, Father John Flynn maintains that parents must know whether their children are getting contraceptives, arguing that parents' right to protect and guide their children outweighs the children's right to privacy. He contends that parents' authority is undermined by allowing children to obtain birth control without their knowledge or permission. Flynn finds it ironic that certain state laws require underage teenagers to get parental permission for a tanning salon, but not necessarily for contraception. Flynn wrote this article for Catholic Online.

As you read, consider the following questions:

1. According to Flynn, what is parental notification? Parental consent?

Father John Flynn, "Undermining Parents: Access to Abortion and Contraception by Minors," Catholic.Org, November 13, 2007. Reproduced by permission. Article provided by Catholic.org.

2. What kind of impact did laws requiring parental involvement have on abortion rates for minors, according to the author?

3. What did King Middle School in Portland, Maine, do on October 18, 2007?

The authority of parents in caring for their children received a blow recently when the Alaska Supreme Court ruled that underage girls can seek abortions without parental consent. According to a Nov. 3 [2007] report by the Associated Press, the ruling upheld a Superior Court decision finding the 1997 Parental Consent Act to be unconstitutional.

In the ruling explaining the 3-2 decision, Chief Justice Dana Fabe stated that while they did agree the Constitution does permit a scheme that provides for parental notification, the law in question violated a minor's right to privacy.

By contrast, Justice Walter Carpeneti, who wrote the dissenting opinion, said that the act did balance the right to privacy with the state's interest in protecting children and the parents' right to guide their children.

Alaska's governor, Sarah Palin, described the judgment as "outrageous," according to the Associated Press. "The State Supreme Court has failed Alaska by separating parents from their children during such a critical decision, moving in the exact opposite direction from the law's intent," she commented.

According to a study by Stateline.org, a Washington, D.C.-based news service, states have passed two types of laws regarding abortion and parental involvement. The first requires one or both parents to approve the procedure, while the second merely requires doctors to notify parents before performing an abortion for a minor.

Overall, as of June 11 [2007] when the information was last updated, 22 states enforce parental consent laws requiring at least one parent to sign a statement approving the procedure. Another 12 states enforce parental notification laws. Utah enforces both consent and notification laws.

Parent Involvement Reduces Number of Abortions

The laws have, however, run into legal problems in some states. In nine states, courts have rejected parental involvement statutes for violating privacy and equal-protection clauses in their state constitutions.

The usefulness of the parental consent laws on abortion was analyzed in a report published Feb. 5 by the Heritage Foundation. Michael J. New, an assistant professor of political science at the University of Alabama, found that laws requiring the involvement of parents reduced the abortion rate of minors by an average of 16%.

Another type of pro-life legislation, restricting the public funding of abortion for underage girls, also notably reduced the abortion rate.

New argued that the importance of such pro-life legislation is often overlooked in explaining the decline of abortion among adolescents. Between 1985 and 1999, the minor abortion rate fell by almost 50%, compared with a 29% decline in the overall abortion rate. "While a number of factors may have contributed to this decline, the impact of pro-life legislation on the incidence of abortion among minors cannot be overlooked," he stated.

Don't Give Out Contraceptives at School

Many countries are increasingly making it easy for schoolgirls to receive contraceptives, without informing parents. In England, the *Telegraph* newspaper reported on Oct. 30 that almost one in six 15-year-old girls were given contraception last year, even though at that age they were too young to legally have sex.

According to the article, 50,000 girls aged 15 attended contraception clinics in 2006–07, along with another 31,000 aged 13 or 14. The data came from the Information Center for Health and Social Care.

Mike Judge, a spokesman for the Christian Institute, commented on the statistics in the *Telegraph*. He urged giving them moral guidance and support, instead of distributing contraceptives. "Most women who look back on their teenage years regret starting sexual activity so early," he added.

Another report by the *Telegraph*, published July 9, explained that girls as young as 11 can obtain the morning-after pill at school without telling their parents. The pills are available at sexual health clinics in secondary schools in England, which are being set up as part of a drive to cut teenage pregnancy.

In the United States, meanwhile, school officials in the state of Maine defended their decision to allow children as young as 11 to obtain contraceptives, reported the Associated Press on Oct. 18 [2007]. Portland's King Middle School will become the first middle school in Maine to make a full range of contraception available, including birth control pills and patches.

Although students would need parental permission to use the city-run health center in the school, they wouldn't have to tell them they were seeking birth control.

Sex with a non-spousal minor under 14 is considered gross sexual assault in Maine. According to the Associated Press, officials said it was unclear whether nurses at the health center would be required to report such activities.

The clinics at Portland high schools have offered oral contraceptives for years, reported the *New York Times* on Oct. 21 [2007]. Douglas Gardner, the city's director of health and human services, explained that health officials decided to extend their availability to middle school after learning that 17 middle school students had become pregnant in the last four years.

Don't Let Children Make Adult Decisions

[In 2007, King Middle School in Portland, Maine, started a program where a] child can receive birth control just by asking, and parents are only notified with the child's permission. What happened to the parents' rights? These children are not legal adults and should not be allowed to make such crucial health decisions without parental consent. An eleven year old cannot even go to an R rated movie without being accompanied by a parent, but it seems they are being allowed to make some R rated decisions.

Nathan Penland, "Eleven Year Olds Having Sex, Why Not?"
www.theindependentutsa.com, October 29, 2007.

The article reported that about a quarter of school-based clinics, most of them in high schools, provide some type of contraception.

Parents' Authority Is Undermined

Bishop Richard Malone of Portland said he was shocked by the decision, reported the *Boston Globe* on Oct. 20 [2007]. The Catholic prelate argued that the move would inevitably lead to more sexual experimentation among younger children.

He also expressed concern over the undermining of parents: "When contradictory messages are given to children from important authority figures such as parents and school officials, it can create more confusion and difficulty for children themselves in making this important life decision."

Apart from undermining parents, the move to spread contraceptive use among schoolchildren comes when many question marks exist over their safety.

An advisory panel of gynecologists, obstetricians and other experts told the U.S. Food and Drug Administration that manufacturers should collect more data on the potential side effects of birth control pills and other hormonal contraceptives after they reach the market, reported Reuters on Jan. 24 [2007]. Nevertheless, panel members added that drug companies were unlikely to initiate such studies because of high costs and the potential to uncover negative effects.

Birth Control May Harm Children's Health

A consumer body, the Public Citizen Health Research Group, also pressured for more research on safety problems, reported the *New York Times* on Feb. 13 [2007]. Earlier this year the group petitioned the Food and Drug Administration to ban several popular low-dose oral contraceptives containing desogestrel, a synthetic form of the hormone progestin.

According to the article, the group cited more than a dozen studies indicating that these pills were linked to blood clots in women more often than older versions, which used different forms of progestin.

In an article published May 2 [2007], Andrea Mrozek, manager of research at the Institute of Marriage and Family Canada, wrote about the cancer risks of contraceptives. A meta-analysis conducted by Dr. Chris Kahlenborn, a Pennsylvania-based internist, shows that being on the pill at a young age, before having children, increases the chance of developing breast cancer by an average of 44%, Mrozek wrote.

Kahlenborn's work was published late last year in the peer-reviewed journal of the world-renowned Mayo Clinic.

Ironically a Stateline.org report dated March 27 [2007] noted the tendency toward laws banning minors from activities such as smoking, drinking, and going to indoor tanning salons, due to health concerns.

This year, Utah and Virginia joined 25 other states in placing limits on teens using tanning beds, due to worries about cancer. Most of the laws, Stateline.org reported, require under-age teens to get a parents' permission, but some states completely ban the salons for minors.

The article added that a number of other states are considering similar legislation. A culture that bans tanning, but gives the green light for contraception and abortion for school-age girls has indeed lost sight of what is important.

> *"Mandating parental involvement for contraception could backfire, driving young people to have unprotected sex and putting their health and lives at increased risk."*

Teenagers Should Not Need Their Parents' Permission to Obtain Birth Control

Rebecca Wind

Rebecca Wind is a senior communications associate with the Guttmacher Institute, a sexual and reproductive health think tank. In the following viewpoint, she contends that teens will continue to have sex and will simply do so without contraception if laws require parental consent or notification to obtain birth control. Citing studies, Wind argues that parental permission does not mean that teenagers will necessarily go to their parents for help or advice; it just means that they will have unsafe sex that can lead to STDs or unwanted pregnancies.

As you read, consider the following questions:

1. According to Rebecca Wind, how many teenage girls would stop coming to a health clinic if their parents knew they needed birth control?

Rebecca Wind, "New Studies Signal Dangers of Limiting Teen Access to Birth Control, Information and Services," Guttmacher.org, January 18, 2005. Reproduced by permission of Alan Guttmacher Institute.

2. According to a study cited by the author, what kind of connection has been found between teens' positive attitudes about birth control and pregnancy?

3. How many teenagers does the Guttmacher Institute estimate become pregnant each year?

Laws limiting teenagers' access to contraceptive services and information fail to reduce sexual activity and increase the risk of unintended pregnancy and sexually transmitted diseases (STDs), according to two studies released this week and soon-to-be-published data discussed in a January 18 [2005] audio news briefing sponsored by The Alan Guttmacher Institute. During the briefing, adolescent health experts and policy analysts urged legislators to consider these findings before voting to require parental notification for contraception or supporting additional funding for abstinence-only education programs.

According to new nationally representative data published in the *Journal of the American Medical Association*, roughly one in five teenagers would have unsafe sex if their parents had to be notified when they got birth control at a family planning clinic. Researchers surveyed more than 1,500 female adolescents under age 18 seeking sexual health services, including contraception, at publicly funded family planning clinics in 33 states. They found that three in five had parents who already knew about their clinic visit—typically because teenagers told them or their parents suggested it. But among those whose parents were unaware, 70% would stop coming to the clinic, and a quarter would continue to have sex but would either rely on withdrawal or not use any contraception. Only 1% of all teens surveyed said they would stop having sex.

Unsafe Sex Because of Parental Consent

"It's good news that most teens are talking to their parents about sexual health and birth control, but that doesn't make it good public policy to force them into it," said Rachel Jones, Ph.D., Senior Research Associate at The Alan Guttmacher Institute. "Mandating parental involvement for contraception could backfire, driving young people to have unprotected sex and putting their health and lives at increased risk."

Already, two states (Texas and Utah) require parental consent for state-funded family planning services, and a similar restriction is in place in one Illinois county where research has found an increase in teen birthrates while other counties experienced declines. Last year, bills to impose new requirements for parental consent for adolescents seeking contraception were introduced in Congress and several states, including Kentucky, Minnesota and Virginia.

"As a pediatrician, every day I see firsthand what happens to teenagers when they can't get contraception and can't discuss it with their parents," said Vinny Chulani, M.D., director of the Division of Adolescent Medicine at the Orlando Regional Medical Center. "We have to face the reality that a majority of teens will have sex by age 18, so we need to do more to help prepare them to have healthy relationships—including providing information on how to talk to their parents and their partners about condoms and birth control and how to use these methods effectively," Dr. Chulani continued. "If we don't, we have no one but ourselves to blame for our nation's high rates of teen pregnancy and STDs."

Positive Attitude Toward Birth Control Encourages Its Use

Teenagers' risks of pregnancy and disease are also affected by what they think about sex, contraception and pregnancy, researchers reported. According to a study just published in *Perspectives on Sexual and Reproductive Health*, the more positive sexually experienced teens' attitudes about birth control, the more likely they are to use it and the less likely to become pregnant. But sexually experienced teens' attitudes toward

When Telling Your Parents Is Not an Option

Many young women live in nontraditional situations—with one parent, a stepparent, other relatives, or on their own. Contact with biological parents, if required by law, may be impossible.

Some teens face violence or other severe consequences from parents as a result of informing their parents that they are seeking contraceptive services. Minors fearful of retribution may forgo using contraception altogether, even though they are already sexually active.

Teens who seek contraceptive services are generally sexually active already. They benefit from meeting with health care providers, who can provide screening, counseling about sexually transmitted diseases, and education about other reproductive health concerns.

Center for Reproductive Rights,
"Parental Consent and Notice for Contraceptives
Threatens Teen Health and Constitutional Rights,"
November 2006, www.reproductiverights.org.

pregnancy are not associated with whether they become pregnant. The authors—Yale University's Hannah Bruckner, Ph.D., and Columbia University's Peter Bearman, Ph.D.—conclude that programs promoting positive attitudes toward contraceptive use, rather than ones focusing solely on the negative consequences of becoming pregnant, may be most effective at reducing teen pregnancies.

Dr. Bearman also reported on an analysis of young adults who had pledged as teenagers to remain virgins until marriage, a type of program that is supported by federal policy. The researchers found that young adults who took virginity pledges as teenagers had the same rates of STDs as other young adults once they became sexually active—even though pledgers had shorter periods of sexual activity and fewer sexual partners. Virginity pledgers are also less likely to know their STD status—increasing the chances they will infect a partner or suffer long-term health consequences. This is of particular concern since nearly nine in ten virginity pledgers have sexual intercourse before getting married.

Dr. Bearman noted that young people's views are increasingly shaped by programs that teach them they must stay abstinent until marriage, while discussing contraceptives only in terms of failure rates. Federal law prohibits government-funded abstinence-only programs from providing information about the health benefits of using contraception, including condoms. "It's truly shocking how little medically accurate information teens are getting about how to protect themselves from pregnancy and disease," he said. "The scare tactics and negative messaging used by today's abstinence-only sex education programs put young people in harm's way."

Abstinence Programs Use Ineffective Scare Tactics

According to a December 2nd [2006] report by Rep. Henry Waxman (D-CA) and the minority staff of the House Committee on Government Reform, the most widely used curricula in federally funded abstinence-only programs are rife with medical inaccuracies, fear-based messages and religious overtones. The U.S. Department of Health and Human Services also released new national data last month showing that while more teens are waiting to have sex and using birth control when they do, many say they are not learning about contraception at school or at home.

Analysts are predicting that social issues—including policies related to teen sexual behavior and reproductive health—will be high on the legislative agenda in the wake of the 2004 elections. "Several new members of the U.S. Senate have built their reputations on being aggressive advocates for restricting government funding for family planning and limiting birth control information," said Cynthia Dailard, senior public policy associate at the Alan Guttmacher Institute.

"In recent years, opponents of family planning have also increased their ranks in state governments, and many have already announced their plans to introduce a wide range of bills that would restrict access to reproductive health services."

As the new Congress and state legislatures get to work in the coming months, policy makers are expected to grapple with the contentious issue of whether teenagers should have confidential access to reproductive health services—including contraception. And debates over what teens should be taught about sex and contraception will continue in many communities across the country. These new findings add to a growing body of evidence that supports making family planning services available to teenagers and providing them with medically accurate, age-appropriate instruction on both how to delay first sex and, for those teens who are sexually experienced, how to consistently, correctly use contraception.

Although the rate of teen pregnancy has dropped over the last decade, the Alan Guttmacher Institute estimates that nearly 850,000 teenagers still get pregnant each year—and the vast majority of these pregnancies are unintended. Nationwide, roughly half of all unintended pregnancies occur among the small proportion of women who are not using any form of birth control. Teenagers also remain at relatively high risk for STDs, accounting for approximately 4 million new cases each year, despite recent declines in teen sexual activity and increases in the use of condoms and other contraceptives among those who are sexually active.

Periodical Bibliography

The following articles have been selected to supplement the diverse views presented in this chapter.

Charlotte Allen	"Planned Parenthood's Unseemly Empire," *The Weekly Standard*, October 22, 2007.
Bob Barr	"SAT Doesn't Stand for Sex Aptitude Test," *The Atlanta Journal-Constitution*, October 24, 2007.
L. Brent Bozell III	"Mainers and No-Brainers," The Culture and Media Institute, October 19, 2007. www.cultureandmediainstitute.org.
Most Rev. Wilton D. Gregory	"What I Have Seen and Heard," *The Georgia Bulletin*, December 30, 2007.
Froma Harrop	"Girls and 'The Pill,'" Real Clear Politics, October 30, 2007. www.realclearpolitics.com.
Randye Hoder	"Sex Education for Parents Too," *Los Angeles Times*, February 13, 2006.
Warren Mass	"'Normalizing' Premarital Sex," *The New American*, January 22, 2007.
James A. Michener	"Sex Education: A Success in Our Social-Studies Class," *The Clearing House*, May-June 2006.
Beth Neil	"Why I Put My Daughter on the Pill at 13," *The Mirror*, September 12, 2007.
David Nova	"Urge Abstinence, But Teach Protection," *The Roanoke Times*, December 6, 2007.
Cindy Rodriguez	"Kids Need to Know the Facts About Sex," *Denver Post*, April 1, 2007.
Michelle Steinberg	"Defeating a Law Harmful to Teens," Planned Parenthood, June 19, 2006. www.plannedparenthood.org.

What Should Teens Be Taught About Birth Control?

Chapter Preface

A new wrinkle was added to the debate over the health benefits and risks of contraceptives and teen sex when Gardasil, a vaccine for four kinds of the human papillomaviruses (HPV), was approved by the U.S. Food and Drug Administration (FDA) in 2006. These four types of HPV are responsible for most of the cases of genital warts and cervical cancer.

According to the FDA's Web site, "For women who do develop cervical cancer, HPV is generally the root cause." Approximately 11,070 women will contract cervical cancer in the United States in 2007, and about 3,870 women will die from the disease, estimates the American Cancer Society.

The FDA has recommended that girls and women between the ages of nine and twenty-six be vaccinated with Gardasil. The U.S. Centers for Disease Control and Prevention (CDC) states that "genital HPV is the most common sexually transmitted infection (STI) in the United States." The CDC also estimates that about 20 million Americans have HPV and that about 6.2 million more will contract it every year. In 2007, according to the National Council of State Legislatures, legislation that would make the HPV vaccine a requirement for school was introduced in twenty-four states and the District of Columbia.

Much of the discussion about teens, contraceptives, and any possible health issues mirrors the debate about abstinence and prevention. The arguments over the FDA's approval of the HPV vaccine for girls as young as nine fall along the same lines.

Advocates of abstinence maintain that teens can avoid HPV and other STIs, as well as AIDS and HIV, only by refraining from having sex until they are married. They are critical of state laws that would make the vaccine mandatory and usurp parents' rights to make decisions for their daughters.

Abstinence supporters worry that this vaccine will encourage promiscuity and lead to fewer women having regular Pap exams. There are concerns about whether the vaccine has been tested long enough to see all unexpected side effects; there also are questions about how long the immunity lasts.

In the *Denver Post* on March 22, 2007, Sigrid Fry-Revere of the Cato Institute writes, "What if the vaccine lulls young women into a false sense of security? Gardasil only protects against the viruses responsible for 70 percent of cervical cancers, and women may not realize the necessity of regular Pap tests even when they've been vaccinated. As a result, many pre-cancerous conditions may go undetected before it is too late."

Opponents of abstinence contend that it is unrealistic to expect all teens to faithfully remain abstinent under all situations and that the vaccine should be used because it can help prevent cervical cancer. In the *New York Times* on May 15, 2007, Jane Brody writes, "Why would this vaccine give girls license to be sexually indulgent? It protects against only one sexually transmitted problem, and there are so many others, including Chlamydia, trichomonoiasis, HIV, and, of course, unwanted pregnancy."

As is the case with the debate over the merits of the HPV vaccine, the debate over the effects of birth control on teens continues with abstinence advocates arguing that only abstinence can completely protect teens' health, while contraception advocates maintain that teens must be fully aware of all their choices because many teens will not choose abstinence. The authors in the following chapter present a variety of viewpoints that examine the role that birth control plays in the health of teens.

> *"A National Institutes of Health panel that included anti-condom advocates examined the effectiveness of condoms from just about every perspective, including strength and porosity; according to its report, released in July 2001, latex condoms are impermeable to even the smallest pathogen."*

Condoms Prevent HIV/AIDS and Sexually Transmitted Diseases

Katha Pollitt

In the following viewpoint, Katha Pollitt argues that the Pope's discouragement of condom use is destructive, because condoms offer the best protection against STDs, HIV, and pregnancy. She maintains, according to a 2002 Human Rights Watch report on abstinence-only sexual education in Texas, a condoms-don't-work campaign led sexually active teens to having unprotected sex. Pollitt also contends that arguing that condoms are ineffective in order to discourage their use is immoral. Pollit's writing has appeared in many publications, including The New Yorker, Harper's Magazine, Ms., *and the* New York Times.

As you read, consider the following questions:

1. According to Katha Pollitt, what is the best protection against sexually transmitted diseases?
2. Who is the new authority on condoms, in the opinion of the author?
3. How is the Pope's stance on condom use damaging, according to the viewpoint?

There are many things to be said against condoms, and most people reading this have probably said them all. But at least they work. Not perfectly—they slip, they break, they require more forethought and finesse and cooperation and trust than is easy to bring to sex every single time, and, a major drawback in this fallen world, they place women's safety in the hands of men. But for birth control they are a whole lot better than the rhythm method or prayer or nothing, and for protection from sexually transmitted diseases they are all we have. This is not exactly a controversial statement; people have been using condoms as a barrier against disease as long as rubber has been around (indeed, before—as readers of James Boswell's journals know). You could ask a thousand doctors—ten thousand doctors—before you'd find one who said, "Condoms? Don't bother."

Abstinence-Only Message May Cause More Harm than Good

But what do doctors know? Or the Centers for Disease Control, or the World Health Organization, or the American Foundation for AIDS Research? These days, the experts on condoms are politicians, preachers and priests, and the word from above is: Condoms don't work. That is what students are being taught in the abstinence-only sex ed favored by the religious right and funded by the Bush administration—$117 million of your annual tax dollars at work. The theory is that even mentioning condoms, much less admitting that they dra-

Condoms Prevent HIV

• The condom—latex or polyurethane, male or female—is the only technology available to prevent the sexual transmission of HIV.

• Laboratory studies show that latex condoms provide an essentially impermeable barrier to particles the size of HIV and other STI pathogens. Studies show that polyurethane condoms also provide effective barriers against sperm, bacteria, and viruses such as HIV.

• Several studies clearly show that condom breakage rates in this country are less than two percent. Most of the breakage and slippage is likely due to incorrect use rather than to the condoms' quality.

Sue Alford, "Condom Effectiveness,"
Advocates for Youth, Sept. 2005.

matically reduce the chances of pregnancy or HIV infection, sends a "mixed message" about the value of total abstinence until marriage. How absurd—it's like saying that seat belts send a mixed message about the speed limit or vitamin pills send a mixed message about vegetables. Anti-condom propaganda can backfire, too: True, some kids may be scared away from sex although probably not until marriage; others, though, hear only a reason to throw caution to the winds. According to a 2002 Human Rights Watch report on abstinence-only sex ed in Texas, a condoms-don't-work ad campaign led sexually active teens to have unprotected sex: "My boyfriend says they don't work. He heard it on the radio." Why is the Bush Administration giving horny teenage boys an excuse to be sexually selfish? You might as well have high school teachers telling them using a condom during sex is like taking a shower in a raincoat.

Now it seems the Vatican is joining fundamentalist Protestants to spread the word against condoms around the globe. "To talk of condoms as 'safe sex' is a form of Russian roulette," said Alfonso Lopez Trujillo, head of the Vatican's office on the family. On the BBC *Panorama* program "Sex and the Holy City," Lopez Trujillo explained, "The AIDS virus is roughly 450 times smaller than the spermatozoon. The spermatozoon can easily pass through the 'net' that is formed by the condom." That latex has holes or pores through which HIV (or sperm) can pass is a total canard. A National Institutes of Health panel that included anti-condom advocates examined the effectiveness of condoms from just about every perspective, including strength and porosity; according to its report, released in July 2001, latex condoms are impermeable to even the smallest pathogen. Among STDs, HIV is actually the one condoms work best against. "We're all a bit stunned by Lopez Trujillo's lack of respect for scientific consensus," Dr. Judith Auerbach of AmfAR [American Foundation for AIDS Research], who sat on the NIH [National Institutes of Health] panel, told me. "Where do his numbers come from?" Is Lopez Trujillo, who even suggests putting warnings on condoms like those on cigarettes, a loose cannon such as can be found in even the best regulated bureaucracies? According to "Sex and the Holy City," in Africa, where HIV infects millions—20 percent in Kenya, 40 percent in Botswana, 34 percent in Zimbabwe—Catholic clergy, who oppose condoms as they do all contraception, are actively promoting the myth that condoms don't prevent transmission of the virus and may even spread it. The *Guardian* quotes the archbishop of Nairobi, Raphael Ndingi Nzeki, as saying: "AIDS . . . has grown so fast because of the availability of condoms." Thus is a decade of painstaking work to mainstream and normalize condom use undone by the conscious promotion of an urban legend.

Time For a Change

When the Nobel Prize for Peace was awarded to Shirin Ebadi, the first ever to a Muslim woman, an Iranian and a crusader for women's rights, not everyone was thrilled. What about Pope John Paul II, now celebrating the twenty-fifth anniversary of his election, and possibly near death [Pope John Paul II died on April 2, 2005]? "This . . . was his year," wrote David Brooks in his *New York Times* column, a hymn of praise for the Pope as the defender of "the whole and the indivisible dignity of each person." A few pages over, Peter Steinfels said much the same in his religion column: "Is there any other leader who has so reshaped the political world for the better and done it peacefully?" More knowledgeable people than I can debate how much credit the Pope should get for the fall of communism—I always thought it was Ronald Reagan with an unintentional assist from Gorbachev plus the internal collapse of the system itself. With the crucial exception of Poland, the countries in the old Soviet bloc aren't even Roman Catholic, or are so only partially. Whatever his contribution to that historic set of events, though, the Pope is on the wrong side of history now. Women's equality, sexual rights for all, the struggle of the individual against authoritarian religion and of course the global AIDS epidemic—the Pope has been a disaster on all these crucial issues of our new century. It's all very well for David Brooks to mock those who critique the Pope for his "unfashionable views on abortion," as if 78,000 women a year dying in illegal procedures around the world was just something to chat about over brie and chablis. But add it up: a priesthood as male as the Kuwaiti electorate—even altar girls may be banned soon, according to one recent news story—no divorce, no abortion, no contraception, no condom use even within a faithful marriage to prevent a deadly infection.

It's bad enough to argue that condoms are against God's will while millions die. But to maintain, falsely, that they are ineffective in order to discourage their use is truly immoral. If not insane.

| "The bottom line is that there's no such thing as safe sex."

Abstinence Prevents HIV/AIDS and Sexually Transmitted Diseases

Shepherd Smith

Shepherd Smith is the president and founder of the Institute for Youth Development, a nonpartisan, nonprofit group that promotes positive behaviors and choices for children. In the following viewpoint, Smith argues that teens need to be made aware that condoms cannot fully protect them from the lifelong health dangers posed by sexually transmitted diseases (STDs), HIV, and other viruses. He contends that abstinence is the best protection against these infections. Smith maintains that teens are being taught and mistakenly believe that condoms can prevent these infections. This article was published in the Institute's The Youth Connection.

As you read, consider the following questions:

1. According to Shepherd Smith, how many teenage girls do not show symptoms of such infections as herpes, chlamydia, and hepatitis B?

Shepherd Smith, "STDs: A Teenage Epidemic?" The *Youth Connection*, March-April 2004. Copyright 2004 The Institute for Youth Development. Reproduced by permission.

2. To which cancer is human papilloma virus (HPV) linked, according to the author?

3. In Shepherd's opinion, what message should teens be hearing from their parents, schools, and communities about sex?

Twenty five years ago, who would have thought that teenage sex could have life-threatening consequences? Not that an unwanted pregnancy or an STD such as gonorrhea or syphilis that was prevalent then isn't a tremendous challenge to a teenager's life, but the stakes are now much higher.

In some ways, we are experiencing a silent invasion. There are no huge headlines on magazine covers and no public service initiatives to highlight the increasingly serious threat facing our teens.

For many of us, this has occurred because of two false perceptions. The first is that there are a limited number of STDs out there, and that apart from HIV/AIDS few, if any, are life-threatening. The second is that as long as we practice "safe sex" we are indeed safe.

Nothing could be further from the truth.

Increase in the Number of STDs

The numbers associated with this epidemic are simply staggering. In June 2000, the National Institutes of Health's Institute of Allergy and Infectious Diseases reported that more than 65 million people in the U.S. are living with an STD—the majority of which are incurable viral infections. That's nearly 25% of the U.S. population, and the number continues to grow.

The numbers seem to be increasing. During the year 2000, approximately 18.9 million new cases of STDs occurred with young people aged 15–24, accounting for 9.1 million cases. Interestingly enough, these numbers may be conservative because not all teens experience symptoms, and therefore, are not diagnosed and counted.

Some researchers believe that as many as 80% of teens with STDs never seek medical attention because they do not notice or recognize symptoms. A study of teen girls who had one or more infections of herpes, chlamydia, gonorrhea, syphilis, and hepatitis B indicated that 87% did not exhibit symptoms. Some teens who do experience symptoms may choose not to be treated because of fear or embarrassment.

Not only is the number of infections large and growing, so are the types of STDs.

For starters, STD is short-hand for somewhere between 25 and 50 different types of sexually-transmitted diseases. Diseases that are caused by sexually-transmitted infections range from irritating but treatable to life threatening.

In addition to the more well-known STDs such as syphilis, chlamydia, herpes, and gonorrhea, there are new viral strains that are not talked about in the mainstream press and are, therefore, not well known. Overall, viruses are particularly troublesome because they are incurable. Once you've contracted a virus, it's up to the immune system to suppress it or allow it to grow. Viruses are spreading like wildfire.

Viruses That Are Incurable

The human papilloma virus (HPV) is a potentially deadly disease that is incurable. There are more than 100 different strains in existence today. HPV is directly linked to 99.7% of all cervical cancer. HPV-related cancer kills more women in the U.S. today than HIV/AIDS.

In 2000, HPV infection accounted for approximately 6.2 million of all sexually-transmitted diseases among Americans aged 15–44. It is estimated that 74% occurred among 15–24 year-olds. It also accounts for 45% of the total medical cost for all STDs in the U.S. The total annual STD cost in the U.S. is estimated to be $6.5 billion.

A variety of studies have shown that after their first sexual contact, girls have a 46% chance of contracting HPV. A recent study revealed that 50% of sexually-active females between 18 and 22 have HPV. Gynecologists throughout the country are reporting that they are seeing an alarming number of pre-cancerous conditions among girls who are in their teens and early 20s.

Equally alarming is that approximately 20% of our population over the age of 12 has the herpes type 2 virus. The U.S. Centers for Disease Control and Prevention believe the number could be as large as 45 million plus people. There has been a 500% increase in herpes type 2 in white teens since 1976. It is estimated that teens aged 15–24 acquire 640,000 new herpes type 2 infections each year. Herpes type 2 causes genital infections, but it can also infect the mouth. Symptoms can be treated, but like HPV, it is an incurable virus that retreats into the nerve cells and then randomly recurs—sometimes with great frequency.

Herpes type 2 is very contagious. While most people become infected when the other partner is having an outbreak, it is believed that the virus can shed cells in between outbreaks, thereby causing infections when no symptoms are present.

Overall, herpes can be a very painful, disruptive, and psychologically damaging disease for teens, their future mates and their unborn children. In addition to uncomfortable outbreaks, a female who has a first episode of herpes type 2 while pregnant can pass it along to her baby. This can cause premature births, nerve damage, and other serious problems that affect the brain, skin and eyes of the child.

And then, there's HIV/AIDS. While most people are familiar with this disease, it is not widely known that a person can be infected and contagious before a blood test detects the antibodies that are present as a result of the virus. This should be a very sobering fact for teens and adults alike as they make decisions about whether they should engage in sexual relationships.

No Such Thing as Safe Sex

So, why is this happening to our youth? What has changed during the past 25 years that has resulted in an overwhelming public health problem for young people?

For starters, young adults are more likely than other age groups to have multiple sex partners, and for young women, to choose sexual partners older than themselves. Research has shown that older sex partners pose a greater risk for teen HIV infection, in particular, because they are more likely to have had multiple partners and a wider variety of sexual and drug experiences.

Young women are biologically more susceptible to chlamydia, gonorrhea, HPV and HIV because their biological system presents more fertile ground for these infections than adult females. As a result, teenage girls are likely to suffer more long-term consequences.

A parent cannot underestimate the fact that teens will increase the number of partners they have when they have sex at earlier ages. Studies indicate that the earlier they begin, the more likely they are to have an increasing number of partners. More partners means increased exposure to infection.

More importantly, many teens have a misguided sense of safety. They have been led to believe they can practice "safe sex" by using condoms and participating in oral sex.

The numbers prove it. Nearly 1 out of 5 teens report that oral sex is safe. In addition, teens have been led to believe that condoms provide safe sex. Many are unaware of the fact that condoms do not effectively reduce their exposure to many STDs. In some cases, they offer no protection at all.

HPV and herpes, for example, can be transmitted in a variety of ways including skin-to-skin contact. Even if a condom is used, infections like these can be transmitted by areas not covered or protected by the condom. In addition, some vi-

No Real Protection From Most Contraceptives

The main purpose of contraceptives is to prevent pregnancy. The main purpose of most contraceptives is NOT to prevent the spread of sexually transmitted diseases. In fact, most contraceptive methods provide absolutely NO protections against STDs. The only contraceptive methods that have proven to provide any protection against STDs are the male condom and, to a limited degree spermicide.

Shelley Ver Steeg,
"Abstinence Is Best Message,"
Daily Herald, *August 9, 2007.*

ruses, including herpes can be transmitted orally. Recent studies indicate that oral herpes now causes 75% of genital herpes vs. 25% in previous years.

Moreover, there is little reason to believe that a sexually active teen would use a condom 100% of the time. Of the teens who report using condoms, approximately 25% report that alcohol or drug use seriously affects their ability to use them correctly. In addition, condoms slip or break 1.6% to 3.6% of the time even when consistently used.

The bottom line is that there's no such thing as safe sex. Even the National Institutes of Health report on condom effectiveness, that was issued in July 2001, highlighted the fact that condoms do not offer high levels of protection against all STDs. It is unfortunate that this report received relatively little attention when it was issued, because it helps parents and youth development professionals realize a better understanding of the STD epidemic and its impact on public health.

Abstinence Is the Best Protection

First, arm yourselves and your children with the facts. Informed decisions will help them make healthier choices. Remind them that antibiotics don't work on everything anymore. Once they contract a virus, they're stuck with it for life.

Understand what's being taught in the schools. Exactly what are your children hearing in the classroom? Are they getting up-to-date information about infection and prevention? Is sexual abstinence offered as a reliable alternative to other methods of birth control and as a 100% effective means to prevent STD infection? Do they understand that even if they find a reliable method of birth control, their new-found sexual freedom becomes a potential gateway to a wide range of diseases and emotional distresses that can turn their lives upside down?

Then, tell your kids to abstain from sex. They want you to do so. Studies consistently show that the majority of teens want to hear these messages from their schools, their religious communities, and most importantly, from their parents. Also explain that sex in itself is not a negative activity. It will become a positive experience with the right person, at the right time, in the right setting such as marriage.

A wide range of studies report that teens rely on their parents' guidance and support more than that of friends, teachers, siblings, girlfriends or boyfriends when they face important decisions or problems. Eight in ten young people report they rely on their parents, while 63% say they rely on parents a lot.

Research has also uncovered that many teens have a predilection for sexual abstinence messages. The majority of teens interviewed in a study funded by the Kaiser Foundation in 2000, for example, indicated that being a virgin is acceptable and even admired among teens. Three-quarters of these teens considered it a good thing to make a conscious decision not to have sex until some later time.

Nearly 94% of teens, responding to a study conducted in 2000 by the National Campaign to Prevent Teen Pregnancy, said it was very important to get strong messages that they abstain from sex until they are at least out of high school. In addition, whether sexually experienced or not, most teens say they are extremely worried about pregnancy, HIV/AIDS and other STDs. In fact, HIV/AIDS is one of the biggest sexual health concerns facing teens.

> *"The group estimates that 200,000 cases of ovarian cancer and 100,000 deaths from the disease have been prevented to date by oral contraception."*

The Pill Can Have Important Health Benefits

Amanda Schaffer

In the following viewpoint, Amanda Schaffer argues that oral contraception does not necessarily negatively affect a woman's health. She cites studies that show that the odds of getting ovarian cancer are lowered the longer a woman is on the Pill, and argues that the Pill will most likely have a more positive effect as less estrogen is used in different formulas. Amanda Schaffer is a science and medical columnist for slate.com, where this article appeared.

As you read, consider the following questions:

1. According to Amanda Schaffer, how many women around the world use oral contraception?
2. As cited by Schaffer, what have studies about nonsmokers and the Pill found?

3. According to the author, how is it possible that the Pill protects a woman against ovarian cancer?

Last week [January 26, 2008], British researchers published decisively good news about birth control pills: They lower the risk of ovarian cancer—substantially. The longer women take the Pill, the lower their odds of getting this kind of cancer. And some of the benefits seem to persist, even decades after women go off the contraception. The new analysis pooled large amounts of data. It was elegantly done. And it's worth celebrating, partly because health claims about the Pill are often much harder to parse.

The Pill Offers Health Benefits

Consider the mental tightrope we've been asked to walk when it comes to the effect of oral contraception on sex drive, cardiovascular disease, and breast cancer: The Pill may sap our libidos (say Scottish doctors)—but it may also be linked to more frequent orgasms (say Italian ones). It increases the risk of blood clots, and may slightly increase the risk of strokes (which remains very small). But it doesn't seem to up the odds of a heart attack, at least for nonsmokers, and might even offer some cardio protection. At the same time, in contrast to the new findings that it protects against ovarian cancer, the Pill may slightly increase the risk of breast cancer. And, then again, it may not, especially when newer formulations with lower doses of estrogen are considered. In other words, oral contraception is a moving target for medical research, and its health history would make for a first-rate feminist rock opera. The grand finale? The Pill gets better with age.

When Margaret Sanger [founder of the American Birth Control League, which eventually became Planned Parenthood] first dreamed of a "magic pill" to prevent unwanted pregnancy, and then its actual appearance came to symbolize sexual and personal freedom for women, few wanted to dwell on tough questions about potential health hazards. But in 1969, journalist Barbara Seaman forced the issue with her book *The Doctor's Case Against the Pill*. Congressional hearings followed, helping to galvanize a feminist backlash against the Pill, and against doctors and medical paternalism in general. Today, though more than 100 million women around the world use oral contraception, suspicion lingers about possible risks like cancer and strokes. And pro-lifers gleefully fan the flames, claiming against all reason and medical evidence that the Pill causes early abortions. All of which is to say that whether new findings about the Pill weigh in for health benefits or for risks, they are always freighted.

Take one evergreen headline: "Does the Pill Make Women Frigid?" In 1995, Scottish researchers found that women taking pills with estrogen and progestin in them reported decreased interest in sex (though women taking progestin-only pills did not). More recently, the idea that women's sex drive is linked to testosterone levels has gained ground. (That's the theory behind the testosterone skin patch, one candidate for Lady Viagra.) Some forms of the Pill seem to indirectly reduce women's blood levels of testosterone—and that decline may persist even after they stop taking the Pill, one study suggests.

But the testosterone story has caveats. Women's sex drive clearly depends on a host of factors, many of them psychological. Surely, the freedom of sex without fear of pregnancy can be a turn-on. And recently, Italian researchers found that women who took birth control pills containing 30 micrograms of estrogen and 3 milligrams of a progestin called drospirenone reported greater sexual enjoyment and greater frequency of orgasm than they did before. Sounds almost like Lady Viagra.

Claims about the Pill and cardiovascular disease also go both ways. In 1961, the *Lancet* reported that a nurse using oral contraception had suffered a pulmonary embolism—the first such report to appear in the literature, according to this

> # Oral Contraceptives Can Prevent Ovarian Cancer
>
> While the average 20-year-old woman may not be thinking about whether she will get ovarian cancer (she is more likely to be concerned about breast and cervical cancer, where the lifetime risk is much higher), a strong message about the overall cancer preventing benefits of oral contraceptives would be a positive public-health message empowering women to decide for themselves about the evidence.
>
> *"The Case for Preventing Ovarian Cancer,"*
> The Lancet, *January 26, 2008.*

2005 review. In the years that followed, several epidemiological studies found that the Pill upped the odds of blood clots, pulmonary embolisms, strokes, and heart attacks (although the risks of these problems remained small). In 1988, for instance, data from the large and prospective Nurses Health Study showed that women taking oral contraception were two and a half times as likely to have heart attacks as women who were not.

Good News for Nonsmokers

More recently, however, research has tried to tease out the impact of the Pill on women who smoke, or have diabetes or hypertension, from its effect on women who don't. The Nurses Health Study concluded that for nonsmokers, the Pill does *not* increase the risk of heart disease. Other studies back this up, as well. And in 2006, researchers at Cedars-Sinai Research Institute, in Los Angeles, found that past use of oral contraception may actually lower women's risk of heart problems. (Still, wild cards like this unpublished study, which turned up higher rates of atherosclerosis in women taking the Pill for extended periods of time, keep everyone on edge.)

And then there is breast cancer. In the mid-1990s, a large meta-analysis linked birth control pills to a small increase in women's odds of getting breast cancer. The increased risk began to decrease again when they stopped taking the Pill, but took 10 years to disappear entirely. By contrast, in 2002, another major study published in the *New England Journal of Medicine* found that use of the Pill was not associated with breast cancer risk, even for women who took it for longer periods of time or used formulations with higher doses of estrogen. Since then, more dueling findings have appeared. In the end, the bottom line tends toward reassurance. Recent evidence suggests that newer pills pose less of a risk than older ones. And a helpful summary published this month argues that when all is said and done, today's birth control pills "do not play a clinically important role in the risk of breast cancer."

Pill Cuts the Risk of Ovarian Cancer

Meanwhile, the news on ovarian cancer has long been consistently good. Friday's findings, published in the *Lancet*, seal the deal. Researchers pooled data from 45 epidemiological studies, including more than 23,000 women with ovarian cancer and more than 87,000 controls. They found that for every five years on the Pill, women's relative risk of ovarian cancer was reduced by 20 percent. After 15 years on the Pill, the risk was cut in half. The Pill probably protects against this kind of cancer because it suppresses ovulation, in which the ovary releases an egg. The group estimates that 200,000 cases of ovarian cancer and 100,000 deaths from the disease have been prevented to date by oral contraception.

Whatever else we don't know about the magic pill, here's to that.

> "Did you know that some forms of birth
> control can make women deathly ill?
> The government knows. But they seem
> to be making a point of being extremely
> silent about that untidy fact."

The Pill Can Be Harmful to Your Health

Judie Brown

In the following viewpoint, Judie Brown argues that birth control pills and patches threaten the lives of the women who use them, yet the risks of using them are ignored by the media and government, particularly with regard to causing blood clots, heart attacks, and strokes in women. She believes this disregard for human life is indicative of American society's attitude toward life in general. Brown is the president and cofounder of the America Life League, a Catholic, prolife, educational grassroots group.

As you read, consider the following questions:

1. According to Judie Brown, how does a birth control patch affect the circulatory system?
2. What is the number one killer of American women, according to the author?

3. In Brown's opinion, how are the three headlines cited by her examples of how humans are being dehumanized?

A ll too often lately, reading the news gives me the chills.

We live in a world that is upside down, yet far too few people seem to care. And that troubles me. We go along, doing what we do, never stopping to question the media reports that suggest this topsy-turvy reality is the proper direction for culture, our nation and our very lives.

Here's what I mean. Did you know that there are great apes and chimpanzees that will shortly be walking around with human brain cells in their little craniums? There was a time when ethical research scientists told the public that such a vision of "Planet of the Apes" would never happen. Not so, says a group of academics assembled by Johns Hopkins University.

Oh, not to worry, these little human-apes won't be passing through the subway turnstiles any time soon, but watch out. When scientists start telling us that something they are thinking about could never be done without the strictest of guidelines, it a sure-fire bet that they are already wondering where to get started. There are far too many scientists who think if something can be done, it should be done—ethical considerations notwithstanding.

In case that little tidbit doesn't curl your toes, try the next one. Did you know that some forms of birth control can make women deathly ill? The government knows. But they seem to be making a point of being extremely silent about that untidy fact.

Tell the Truth About the Risks

Ortho-Evra manufactures a birth control patch, and even advertises it on television. The ad doesn't get very specific about how it works, though. The patch is loaded with chemicals, and it sticks to the skin. The chemicals—hormones, actually— flow steadily through the skin, into the bloodstream, and throughout the circulatory system. The hormones are the same ones found in the birth control pill, but we're told the delivery system employed by the patch makes it "safer and more effective" than taking a pill.

Or is it? The Associated Press reports "about a dozen" young women in their late teens and early twenties died last year from blood clots believed to be related to this patch. And several lawsuits are pending on behalf of women who either died or developed blood clots while using the patch.

Some experts in the "family planning" field seem to shrug this off, saying a few deaths are bound to happen. As they see it, there is no need to investigate, warn women or otherwise take action to suspend sales of the patch. In fact, many professionals in the birth control field agree that blood clots are an accepted risk from hormonal birth control.

Tell that to the families of those dead women.

The Pill Increases the Risk of Heart Attack or Stroke

As if learning that the patch snuffs out a few of its users isn't bad enough, we also find new reports that low dose birth control pills can increase the user's risk of heart attack or stroke. While this has been pointed out repeatedly over the years, there is new evidence that makes the point a bit stronger than earlier studies. This review focuses on the fact that women who use the Pill for extended periods of time are at a significantly higher risk of cardiovascular problems.

Now remember all those health reports on TV about women and heart disease? The federal government's entire "Heart Truth" campaign, lead by President Bush's wife Laura, is focused on making sure Americans know that heart disease is the number one killer of women. Millions are being spent to raise awareness among women in the United States, and yet

The Pill Increases Risk for Breast Cancer

Looking at 54 studies of the Pill, [Dr. Maria Kraw] observed that researchers found that it caused a 24 percent increased risk of breast cancer. The real tragedy, however, Kraw noted, is that the greatest risk occurs right after early puberty when the breasts are still developing. Taken before a woman's first pregnancy, the hormonal contraceptive has the most negative side-effects.

Elizabeth O'Brien, "Noted Endocrinologist Dispels the Myth of Health Benefits of the Pill, Part 2," LifeSiteNews, August 9, 2007. www.lifesitenews.com.

nowhere on the campaign's Web site is there a warning about birth control hormones and their potential to contribute to the problem.

When birth control researchers and clinicians assure us that there is no need to worry because a few deaths here and there are to be expected, women across the nation should be worried indeed—very worried. What's everybody trying to hide?

Are you getting the impression that all these "expert" scientists are not really leveling with us average folks? If you're still not convinced, I have one more example for you to ponder. For me, at least, this takes the cake.

Dehumanizing Humans

NBC's Katie Couric recently spoke with a California family who resorted to in vitro fertilization [IVF] because they so badly wanted to have a baby. The couple had twins using IVF, and then asked their doctor to freeze the embryos not used in this initial treatment for "later." The doctor proved most untrustworthy. He "misplaced" some of this couple's frozen human embryos, and was even caught selling eggs on the black market. But even after all these shenanigans, which speak volumes about the test-tube baby business, there were still some embryos in the freezer. The couple decided to pursue another round of treatments, and we are told that one of the remaining embryos then "became" the couple's daughter.

The truth is that this specific human embryo already was their daughter, just as she was during the entire time she was in the freezer. In fact, every single one of those frozen embryos, including the "misplaced," are human beings with personal identities.

America is in deep denial that human embryos are human beings. We can now talk freely about doctors who lose babies, misplace babies, and then speak about babies becoming babies. This denial is possible because we really don't believe that a human embryo is a baby; we believe that those "cells" could become a baby! None of the "experts" have the guts to point out that it really does not matter what anybody believes; each human embryo is, and always will be, an individual human being.

Lewis Carroll once put the following words in Humpty Dumpty's mouth: "When I use a word, it means just what I choose it to mean—neither more nor less."

We might likewise say of today's love affair with the persistent dehumanization of human beings, people can be what we want them to be, neither more nor less. The headlines tell the tale:

- Great apes can be partly human, but not quite.

- Young women can be misled because they might get pregnant and are better off being artificially sterile, even if they might grow very ill or even die.

- Human embryos can be useful, but not really human.

175

An old rhyme comes to mind. A bit simple, perhaps, but stunningly accurate: "Oh what tangled webs we weave, when we first practice to deceive." Cruel cunning indeed!

> *"Access to the drug over-the-counter, or without a prescription, would prompt use among consumers who, unknowingly, have medical conditions that put them at high risk of life-threatening complications."*

The Morning-After Pill Does More Harm Than Good

Wendy Wright

Wendy Wright is the president of Concerned Women for America, a women's organization that focuses on public policy issues. In the following viewpoint, she maintains that the morning-after pill (MAP) should be sold only with a prescription. Wright believes that allowing easy access to the pill will lead only to health risks for women. These include preexisting health conditions that could lead to complications, men who have given the drug to women without their consent, an increase in the number of STDs, and more unsafe sex.

As you read, consider the following questions:

1. According to Wendy Wright, how many women between the ages of 18 and 44 have diabetes? How many do not know that they have it?

Wendy Wright, "Talking Points on the Morning-After Pill," Cwfa.org, August 24, 2006. Reproduced by permission.

2. According to the author, how many Americans believe life begins at fertilization?

3. In what country does the author cite as having an increase in the number of teenage girls using the morning-after pill since it became available in pharmacies?

The morning-after pill (MAP) lacks testing for safety to women. Access to the drug over-the-counter, or without a prescription, would prompt use among consumers who, unknowingly, have medical conditions that put them at high risk of life-threatening complications. It could be slipped to women without their knowledge, and statutory rapists would rely on it to cover up their abuse of adolescents. In areas that allow easy access, the sexually transmitted disease rates have skyrocketed. The drug owner encourages multiple sex partners (putting women at risk of sexually transmitted diseases, or STDs), and endorses frequent use of the drug, though it has not conducted studies on multiple use. Morning-after pill promoters have been found guilty of overstating the efficacy of the drug and understating the risks to women.

MAP Puts Women at Risk

- Over-the-counter access would extend the availability of the MAP to a broader population than any study has included—females who have not been counseled or screened for contraindications.

- Easy access allows someone other than the consumer to buy it and then slip it to a woman without her knowledge or consent. Unlike other drugs like aspirin, there is more potential for abuse by someone who, contrary to or unaware of the woman's wishes, does not want her pregnant. Drugs less easy to administer have been used against women:

In one example, Gary Bourgeois' girlfriend refused to have an abortion. During sexual relations, he inserted misoprostol, used in the RU-486 abortion regimen. Later she experienced violent cramps then felt a partly dissolved pill drop from her vagina. Her baby died. He pleaded guilty to aggravated assault and administering a noxious substance in Canada in September, 2003.

In another incident, Dr. Stephen Pack pleaded guilty to injecting Joy Schepis with an abortion-inducing drug in April 2000. The Bronx, New York, doctor jabbed his former lover with a syringe filled with methotrexate, which causes abortions, because she refused to have one.

- It will be difficult for doctors to treat complications when the woman's medical history is unknown or hidden.

- The morning-after pill is a high dose of the birth control pill, which requires a medical exam, a prescription, and physician oversight. Birth control pills can cause significant or life-threatening conditions such as blood clots, stroke and heart attacks. Birth control pills are contraindicated for women with diabetes, liver problems, heart disease, breast cancer, deep vein thrombosis, and for women who smoke and are over 35. Physician oversight is necessary to ensure that none of these contraindications exists. For example, according to the Centers for Disease Control, approximately 1.85 million women of reproductive age (18–44) have diabetes; approximately 500,000 do not know that they have the disease.

- The World Health Organization has warned: "There may be a higher percentage of ectopic pregnancies among emergency contraceptive pill failure cases than among a normal pregnant population."

- Nurses at the Royal College of Nursing warned that pharmacists in the United Kingdom (where the drug is available behind the counter) were failing to warn customers of possible complications or carry out routine medical assessments.

Scientific Studies Are Needed

- The long-term effects.

- The high dosage. A drug's safety at one dose or range of doses does not mean that the drug is equally safe at a much higher dose. Yet proponents stake their arguments on decades of use of the birth control pill, a lower dose—which is not available over-the-counter.

- Repeated usage. In the United Kingdom, one in seven of all women used the morning-after pill repeatedly in the same year.

- Females not screened for medical contraindications.

- Adolescents.

- The Food and Drug Administration's approval of the morning-after pill with a prescription was not based on controlled scientific studies, but on unscientific, anecdotal evidence. All studies (including those cited in the over-the-counter approval application of Plan B, a brand of the MAP) focus on the drug's relative reliability in decreasing the expected birth rate, not on the effect on the women who have taken the drug regimen.

False Advertising About the Effects of the Drug

- The FDA found Plan B's promoters guilty of false advertising, for overstating efficacy (claiming greater effectiveness in prohibiting pregnancies than the evidence shows) and understating the medical risks to women.

The FDA stated the "ads raise significant public health and safety concerns." Yet proponents continue to make similar claims.

- Plan B's promoters make the contradictory claim that the MAP inhibits implantation but does not end a pregnancy. Nearly half of Americans (46 percent) believe life begins at fertilization. Knowledge that the MAP can terminate a pregnancy could affect a woman's decision to use it; withholding such information violates the principle of informed consent.

- Promoters have relied on junk science to claim it does not affect sexual behaviors. At least one study (from the University of Pittsburgh) included only teenagers already engaged in risky sexual activity, and then concluded that easy access to MAP did not change their behavior.

- The American College of Obstetricians and Gynecologists (ACOG) recommends that low-dose oral contraceptives be available only with a prescription from a licensed health-care provider. Yet it is recommending that Plan B and other higher-dose hormone regimens be available over-the-counter.

- ACOG did not poll its members. Its recommendation is not representative of its members. MAP proponents had complained that doctors have not been willing to hand out the drug to anyone (apparently a driving reason for them to seek over-the-counter status—to bypass medical intervention intended to protect women).

- MAP promoters demonstrate a disturbing lack of concern for women's health:

  Plan B's Web site responds to the question, "How often can Plan B be provided," by stating, "Plan B can be provided as frequently as needed."

No One Knows the Extent of Possible Health Risks Related to the Morning-After Pill

Carole Denner, a registered nurse and legislative director for Concerned Women for America, points out that, "No one has ever followed the women taking the high-dose compound to see if there are problems. There has never been a single long-term, scientific study. And obviously, several serious problems—like blood clots—can arise even with lower doses."

Shaunti Feldhahn, "Morning-After Pill Shouldn't Be on Shelves," The Atlanta Journal-Constitution, February 11, 2004.

The Web site acknowledges the need for intervention and oversight. "Providers can help a client determine whether Plan B treatment makes sense given the timing of unprotected intercourse and her level of concern about an unwanted pregnancy." However, over-the-counter access would eliminate "providers," thereby eliminating the opportunity for counsel, caution, and the screening out of women with contraindications.

The Web site encourages unnecessary use of the MAP for women already taking oral contraceptives—even though women are only fertile within days of ovulation: "Women taking oral contraception do not have true menstrual cycles and are at risk of pregnancy. [E]mergency contraception may be indicated."

- One ad portraying 13 young men with the caption, "So many men. So many reasons to have back up contraception."

- Another pictures a fraternity, with the words, "Delta Delta Thi. 27 upstanding young men. 34 billion sneaky little sperm."

- Another is designed like a poster for adolescents, describing "Damian" as "A Renaissance Guy, a Deep Thinker, an Ancient Soul, a Walking Sperm Factory."

Risks to the Public's Health

- Regions that allow easy access to the MAP experience a significant increase in sexually transmitted diseases. In the United Kingdom, chlamydia cases rose from 7,000 in 1999 to 10,000 cases last year. Gonorrhea cases climbed nearly 50 percent, to nearly 3,000 cases last year, up from 2,000 in 1999. The highest increases were among 16–19 year olds.

- Contrary to proponents' claims, the number of surgical abortions has not declined with easy access to MAP. In some areas, the number of abortions increased.

- In a [United Kingdom] study of users of MAP, four out of the 12 women interviewed said their choice to have unprotected sexual intercourse was influenced by the knowledge that they could obtain the pill from a pharmacy.

- In response to concern that providing the morning-after pill through pharmacists would lead to more unprotected sex, a user of the pill disclosed: "To be honest, in a way, that is what happened to me. I did previously know that X chemist was just over the road and I think, I think if I hadn't have known . . . if I hadn't have known I could have got it so easily, I would have been more careful, to be honest."

Dangers for Teens

- Many teenagers would be less confident in resisting sexual pressure, particularly if easy access to the pill is in the aggressor's arsenal of coercion. It will increase the likelihood of sexual abuse of girls, and that sexual perpetrators will prolong their rapes, undetected.

- Adolescents are unlikely to recognize if they have medical contraindications, less likely to follow directions for administration or to fully understand a medication label. They are less prone to seek medical help if they suffer symptoms of complications after secretly taking the MAP, and would not be aware that it lacks adequate testing.

- Rather than reducing the core problem of young people engaging in sexual activity (which carries life-long consequences), it encourages sexual activity. An official survey revealed that MAP use among teenage girls in the United Kingdom more than doubled since it became available in pharmacies, increasing from one in 12 teenagers to one in five. Among them were girls as young as 12. A girl who said she was 10 years old told the pharmacist "she had already used it four times."

- Even morning-after pill proponents agree that sexually active girls are likely victims of sexual abuse, and interaction with medical professionals is an important defense.

The Alan Guttmacher Institute reported: "The younger women are when they first have intercourse the more likely they are to have had unwanted or nonvoluntary first sex, seven in 10 of those who had sex before age 13, for example."

"The possibility of sexual abuse should be considered routinely in every adolescent female patient who has initiated sexual activity," stated Dr. Joycelyn Elders in the *Journal of the*

American Medical Association. The rush to choose "pregnancy outcome options" may preempt efforts to rule out sexual abuse.

"Sexual abuse is a common antecedent of adolescent pregnancy, with up to 66% of pregnant teens reporting histories of abuse. . . . Pregnancy may also be a sign of ongoing sexual abuse. . . . Boyer and Fine found that of 535 young women who were pregnant, 44% had been raped, of whom 11% became pregnant as a result of the rape. One half of these young women with rape histories were raped more than once."

MAP Helps Men Abuse Women

The Bangkok Post reported disturbing consequences of easy availability of the morning-after pill for the past 15 years, including:

- Random studies showed that men are the most frequent buyers. "They buy the pills for their girlfriends or wives so that they don't have to wear condoms and feel they're at no risk of becoming a father afterwards. Some women I've spoken to said that they didn't even know what they were taking; that the guy just said it was a health supplement," said Nattaya Boonpakdee, program assistant at the Population Council (an agency dedicated to promoting and developing contraception and abortion methods).

- "Although many feminists believe that the morning-after pill gives them more control over their own bodies, it would seem, judging from the few studies conducted so far, that it is actually being used by men to exploit women."

Women Don't Realize It's Not Birth Control

- The FDA Advisory Committee chairman declared the label comprehension study a "failure"—a full one-third of the women did not understand that the morning-after pill is not to be used as a regular form of birth control.

- The committee was presented limited or incomplete information.

- Some committee members displayed a disturbing lack of interest in the potential abuse of women, and of practical reality. These members advocated that the morning-after pill should be placed in stores outside the line of vision of pharmacists, so customers would not be embarrassed about obtaining it. The committee members did not say how they expect customers to pay for it without anyone seeing.

- The FDA has rejected advisory committee recommendations in the past, most recently regarding silicone breast implants. It is only one of the FDA's multiple levels for evaluation.

> *"This all could have been stopped way before this baby was conceived if they had just let me have that damn pill."*

The Morning-After Pill Does More Good Than Harm

Dana L.

In the following viewpoint, Dana L. describes her frustration and anger about needing to have an abortion because she was unable to obtain emergency contraception in time. She argues that her inability to take Plan B and, consequently, becoming pregnant could have affected her health and unborn child as she was taking three medications, including one for high cholesterol, and the chance she might have a baby with health problems because of her age. Dana L., a writer and lawyer who lives in Virginia, wrote this article for The Washington Post. *She did not publish her last name to protect her family's privacy.*

As you read, consider the following questions:

1. According to Dana L., within how much time does Plan B have to be taken after sex to prevent pregnancy?

2. According to Dana L., why are doctors in Virginia allowed to refuse to prescribe Plan B?

3. Why did the author decide not to have an abortion performed in Virginia?

The conservative politics of the [George W.] Bush administration forced me to have an abortion I didn't want. Well, not literally, but let me explain.

I am a 42-year-old happily married mother of two elementary-schoolers. My husband and I both work, and like many couples, we're starved for time together. One Thursday evening this past March, we managed to snag some rare couple time and, in a sudden rush of passion, I failed to insert my diaphragm.

The next morning, after getting my kids off to school, I called my ob/gyn to get a prescription for Plan B, the emergency contraceptive pill that can prevent a pregnancy—but only if taken within 72 hours of intercourse. As we're both in our forties, my husband and I had considered our family complete, and we weren't planning to have another child, which is why, as a rule, we use contraception. I wanted to make sure that our momentary lapse didn't result in a pregnancy.

No Access to Plan B

The receptionist, however, informed me that my doctor did not prescribe Plan B. No reason given. Neither did my internist. The midwifery practice I had used could prescribe it, but not over the phone, and there were no more open appointments for the day. The weekend—and the end of the 72-hour window—was approaching.

But I needed to meet my kids' school bus and, as I was pretty much out of options—short of soliciting random Virginia doctors out of the phone book—I figured I'd take my chances and hope for the best. After all, I'm 42. Isn't it likely my eggs are overripe, anyway? I thought so, especially since my best friend from college has been experiencing agonizing infertility problems at this age.

Weeks later, the two drugstore pregnancy tests I took told a different story. Positive. I couldn't believe it.

Health Risks During Pregnancy

I'm still in good health, but unlike the last time I was pregnant, nearly a decade ago, I'm now taking three medications. One of them, for high cholesterol, is in the Food and Drug Administration's Pregnancy Category X—meaning it's a drug you shouldn't take if you're expecting or even planning to get pregnant. I worried because the odds of having a high-risk pregnancy or a baby born with serious health issues rise significantly after age 40. And I thought of the emotional upheavals that an unplanned pregnancy would cause our family. My husband and I are involved in all aspects of our children's lives, but even so, we feel we don't get enough time to spend with them as it is.

I felt sick. Although I've always been in favor of abortion rights, this was a choice I had hoped never to have to make myself. When I realized the seriousness of my predicament, I became angry. I knew that Plan B, which could have prevented it, was supposed to have been available over the counter by now. But I also remembered hearing that conservative politics have held up its approval.

My anger propelled me to get to the bottom of the story. It turns out that in December 2003, an FDA advisory committee, whose suggestions the agency usually follows, recommended that the drug be made available over the counter, or without a prescription. Nonetheless, in May 2004, the FDA top brass overruled the advisory panel and gave the thumbs-down to over-the-counter sales of Plan B, requesting more data on how girls younger than 16 could use it safely without a doctor's supervision.

Preventing a Married Woman from Using Plan B

Apparently, one of the concerns is that ready availability of Plan B could lead teenage girls to have premarital sex. Yet this concern—valid or not—wound up penalizing an over-the-hill married woman for having sex with her husband. Talk about the law of unintended consequences.

By late August 2005, the slow action over Plan B led the director of the FDA's Office on Women's Health to resign her post. The agency's delay on the draw, she wrote in an e-mail to her colleagues, "runs contrary to my core commitment to improving and advancing women's health." As recently as April 7, Steven Galson, director of the FDA's Center for Drug Evaluation and Research, said that the agency still needed time to work on the issue.

Unfortunately, time was the one thing I didn't have.

Doctors Refusing to Prescribe a Drug

Meanwhile, I hadn't even been able to get Plan B with a prescription that Friday, because in Virginia, health-care practitioners apparently are allowed to refuse to prescribe any drug that goes against their beliefs. Although I had heard of pharmacists refusing to fill prescriptions for birth control on religious grounds, I was dumbfounded to find that doctors could do the same thing.

Moreover, they aren't even required to tell the patient why they won't provide the drug. Nor do they have to provide a list of alternative sources. I had asked the ob-gyn's receptionist if politics was the reason the doctor wouldn't prescribe Plan B for me. She refused to answer or offer any reason, no matter how much I pressed her. By the time I got on the phone with my internist's office and found that he would not fill a Plan B prescription either, I figured it was a waste of time to fight with the office staff. To this day, I don't know why my doctors wouldn't prescribe Plan B—whether it was because of moral opposition to contraception or out of fear of political protesters or just because they preferred not to go there.

Rape Victims Need Emergency Contraception

An estimated 7,000 women and girls are raped every year in Massachusetts. Rape victims who receive emergency contraception within the first 24 hours reduce their risk of pregnancy by roughly 95 percent. Unfortunately, this does not always happen. Many rape survivors do not seek care, and some who do seek it are denied emergency contraception by their providers.

Dianne Luby, "Compassion in the ER,"
Boston Globe, *December 25, 2005.*

In any event, they were also partly responsible for why I was stuck that Friday, and why I was ultimately forced to confront the decision to terminate my third pregnancy.

After making the decision with my husband, I was plunged into an even murkier world—that of finding an abortion provider. If information on Plan B was hard to come by, and practitioners were evasive on emergency contraception, trying to get information on how to abort a pregnancy in 2006 is an even more Byzantine experience.

On the Internet, most of what I found was political in nature or otherwise unhelpful: pictures of what your baby looks like in the womb from week one, and so on.

Calling doctors, I felt like a pariah when I asked whether they provided termination services. Finally, I decided to check the Planned Parenthood Web site to see whether its clinics performed abortions. They did, but I learned that if I had the abortion in Virginia, the procedure would take two days because of a mandatory 24-hour waiting period, which requires that you go in first for a day of counseling and then wait a day to think things over before returning to have the abortion. Because of work and the children, I couldn't afford two days off, so I opted to have the procedure done on a Saturday in downtown D.C. while my husband took the kids to the Smithsonian.

The hidden world of abortion services soon became even more subterranean. I called Planned Parenthood two days in advance to confirm the appointment. The receptionist politely informed me that the organization never confirms appointments, for "security reasons," and that I would have to just show up.

I arrived shortly before 10 a.m. in a bleak downpour, trusting that someone had recorded my appointment. I shuffled to the front door through a phalanx of umbrellaed protesters, who chanted loudly about Jesus and chided me not to go into that house of abortion.

Keep Religion Out of Politics

All the while, I was thinking that if religion hadn't been allowed to seep into American politics the way it has, I wouldn't even be there. This all could have been stopped way before this baby was conceived if they had just let me have that damn pill.

After passing through the metal detector inside the building, I entered the Planned Parenthood waiting room; it was like the waiting room for a budget airline—crammed full of people, of all races, and getting busier by the moment. I was by far the oldest person there (other than one girl's mom). The wait seemed endless. No one looked happy. We were told that the lone doctor was stuck in Cherry Blossom Parade traffic.

He finally arrived, an hour and a half late.

The procedure itself took about five minutes. I finally walked out of the building at 4:30, 6 1/2 hours after I had arrived.

It was a decision I am sorry I had to make. It was awful, painful, sickening. But I feel that this administration gave me practically no choice but to have an unwanted abortion because the way it has politicized religion made it well-nigh impossible for me to get emergency contraception that would have prevented the pregnancy in the first place.

And to think that, all these years after *Roe v. Wade* became the law of the land, this is what our children have to look forward to as they approach their reproductive years.

Periodical Bibliography

The following articles have been selected to supplement the diverse views presented in this chapter.

LaToya Cain	"Planned Parenthood: Leading the Little Ones Astray," Concerned Women for America, December 7, 2007. www.cwfa.org.
Danielle Crittenden	"'Unprotected:' Sexual Freedom Is Damaging to Students, But Health Officials Must Not Judge," *The Wall Street Journal*, December 14, 2006.
Sigrid Fry-Revere	"Vaccination Bill Mutates," *San Jose Mercury News*, July 11, 2007.
Laura Lambert	"Is the Pill Good for You?" Planned Parenthood, January 31, 2005. www.plannedparenthood.org.
Kate O'Beirne	"A Mandate in Texas: The Story of a Compulsory Vaccination and What It Means," *National Review Online*, March 5, 2007. www.nationalreview.com.
Jeremy Olson	"More Teen Births, Little Unity About What to Do: Some See Cause for Alarm After Teen STD, Abortion Rates Also Rose in 2006," *McClatchy-Tribune Business News*, March 30, 2008.
Robert Rector and Kirk A. Johnson	"Virginity Pledgers Have Lower STD Rates and Engage in Fewer Risky Sexual Behaviors," The Heritage Foundation, June 14, 2005. www.heritage.org.
Geraldine Sealey	"An Epidemic Failure: Whatever Happened to Bush's Pledge to Combat AIDS in Africa?" *Rolling Stone*, June 2, 2005. www.rollingstone.com.
USA Today	"Politics, Not Science, Blocks Access to 'Morning-After' Pill," April 18, 2004.

For Further Discussion

Chapter 1

1. Ann Shibler argues that emergency contraception and birth control pills are chemical forms of abortion and that there are actually more chemical abortions than there are surgical abortions. Jesse Mesich maintains that there are fewer unplanned pregnancies—and abortions—because of emergency contraception. Which argument do you think is more persuasive? Why?

2. The Unitarian Universalist Association of Congregations contends that *Griswold v. Connecticut* is not specifically about birth control but is really about the right to privacy. In the opposing viewpoint, Robert P. George and David L. Tubbs maintain that the Supreme Court incorrectly generalized the right to privacy, which led to it being extended to the right to an abortion in *Roe v. Wade*. In which situations do you feel the right to privacy should be allowed? Can you think of any situations in which this right should not be permitted?

Chapter 2

1. Those who believe that employers should not have to include birth control in their prescription-drug plans argue that it is wrong to force everyone to pay for coverage that some might find offensive and not use at all. Sheldon Richman maintains that this is a "violation of conscience" and that government should not enforce what he calls "universal participation" at the expense of an individual's principles. Those who support the idea of contraceptive-equity coverage contend that the health of women and children are affected by unplanned pregnancies and money is saved with such coverage. National Abortion Rights

Action League (NARAL) also argues that not having such coverage is sex discrimination. Which argument do you think makes a stronger case? Use quotes from the viewpoints to support your view.

2. After reading Doug Bandow's viewpoint on whether pharmacists should have the right to refuse to fill birth-control prescriptions, do you believe there is any justification for a pharmacist to refuse to fill a prescription? Why or why not? Use information from Bandow's article to support your statements.

Chapter 3

1. After reading the viewpoints in this chapter, which type of program do you believe can better solve the problem of teen pregnancy and sexually transmitted diseases (STDs)—abstinence education or comprehensive sex education? Justify your views with quotes and information from the viewpoints.

2. After evaluating the two viewpoints on birth control and parental permission, decide whether you think that the need for parental authority outweighs the right of privacy for teens? Use information from John Flynn and Rebecca Wind's viewpoints to support your answer.

Chapter 4

1. After reading the viewpoints in this chapter, do you believe that abstinence or condoms are more effective in preventing AIDS, HIV, and STDs? Explain your reasoning and use quotes from the viewpoints to support your thinking.

2. Dana L.'s viewpoint about having an abortion because she was unable to obtain emergency contraception (EC) in time is written from a personal point of view. Wendy Wright makes her points in her article by detailing the

specific health risks that EC can cause without using a personal anecdote. Which writing style helps to make the viewpoint stronger? Why?

Organizations to Contact

The editors have compiled the following list of organizations concerned with the issues debated in this book. The descriptions are derived from materials provided by the organizations. All have publications or information available for interested readers. The list was compiled on the date of publication of the present volume; the information provided here may change. Be aware that many organizations take several weeks or longer to respond to inquiries, so allow as much time as possible.

Advocates for Youth
2000 M Street NW, Suite 750, Washington, DC   20036
(202) 419-3420 • Fax: (202) 419-1448
E-mail: info@advocatesforyouth.org
Web site: www.advocatesforyouth.org

Advocates for Youth is a national organization that creates programs and supports policies that educate youth about their sexual and reproductive health. The group's mission is help young people make knowledgeable decisions about their sexual health. Its publications include *The History of Federal Abstinence-Only Funding, Myths & Facts About Sex Education,* and *Adolescent Maternal Mortality: An Overlooked Crisis.*

American Life League
PO Box 1350, Stafford, VA   22555
(540) 659-471 • Fax: (540) 659-2586
E-mail: info@all.org
Web site: www.all.org

Founded in 1979, the American Life League is dedicated to opposing abortion. The group also opposes birth control and emergency contraception as forms of chemical abortion, and uses advocacy, petitions, and a variety of action initiatives in support of these beliefs. Publications available from the League include the newsletters *Communiqué, STOPP Report,* and *Rock for Life Report.*

Alan Guttmacher Institute

125 Maiden Lane, 7th Floor, New York, NY   10038
(212) 248-1111 • Fax: (212) 248-1951
E-mail: info@guttmacher.org
Web site: www.guttmacher.org

The Alan Guttmacher Institute is a sexual and reproductive health research group. It uses statistical data and research to protect and expand the reproductive choices for men and women, including birth control and safe and legal abortion. Its publications include the annual *Perspectives on Sexual and Reproductive Health* and *International Family Planning Perspectives* and *State Policies in Briefs*.

Center for Reproductive Rights

120 Wall Street, New York, NY   10005
(212) 637-3600 • Fax: (212) 637-3666
E-mail: info@reprorights.org
Web site: www.reproductiverights.org

The Center for Reproductive Rights is dedicated to ensuring that reproductive freedom remains legal, safe, and accessible. Its goals include supporting access to contraceptives and abortion, and promoting reproductive health care for young people. Its publications include the fact sheet *Emergency Contraception: An Important Component of Women's Rights*, the briefing paper *Adolescents Need Safe and Legal Abortion*, and the book *What If Roe Fell?*

Concerned Women for America (CWA)

1015 Fifteenth Street NW, Suite 1100
Washington, DC   20005
(202) 488-7000 • Fax: (202) 488-0806
Web site: www.cwfa.org

Concerned Women for America (CWA) is a women's organization that is devoted to public policy issues that protect and promote traditional values through education and legislative action. The CWA supports traditional marriage, abstinence, religious liberty, and opposes abortion, pornography, and sex education. It publishes the monthly *Family Voices*.

Family Research Council
801 G Street NW, Washington, DC   20001
(202) 393-2100 • Fax: (202) 393-2134
Web site: www.frc.org

The Family Research Council is devoted to promoting marriage and family. It opposes homosexuality and condom distribution programs in schools, and supports abstinence until marriage. The council publishes such books as *The Top Ten Myths About Abortion and Politicized Science: The Manipulated Approval of RU-486 and Its Dangers to Women's Health*, and such research papers as "*Why Wait: The Benefits of Abstinence Until Marriage*."

The Heritage Foundation
214 Massachusetts Avenue NE
Washington, DC   20002-4999
(202) 546-4400 • Fax: (202) 546-8328
E-mail: info@heritage.org
Web site: www.heritage.org

The Heritage Foundation is a public policy research institute that supports the ideas of limited government, traditional American values, and the free-market system. It promotes the view that the welfare system has contributed to the problems of illegitimacy and teenage pregnancy. Among the Foundation's publications are policy papers on such subjects as *Teenage Sexual Abstinence and Academic Achievement, SCHIP Expansion: More Birth Control for Minors, Less Involvement by Parents*, and *Sex Education—By the Book*.

National Abstinence Education Association
1701 Pennsylvania Avenue NW, Suite 300
Washington, DC   20006
(202) 248-5420 • Fax: (202) 580-6559

E-mail: info@abstinenceassociation.org
Web site: www.abstinenceassociation.org

The National Abstinence Education Association promotes and supports abstinence education. The group lobbies for more abstinence-education funding, conducts research in support of it, and works with local and state organizations to encourage it. Research papers published by the Association include *Straight From the Source: What So-Called "Comprehensive" Sex Education Teaches to America's Youth* and *Abstinence Works!*

National Campaign to Prevent Teen and Unplanned Pregnancy

1776 Massachusetts Avenue NW, Suite 200
Washington, DC   20036
(202) 478-8500 • Fax: (202) 478-8588
Web site: www.thenationalcampaign.org

The National Campaign works to reduce the number of teenage pregnancies and unplanned pregnancies among adults who are young and single. The group supports policies to educate teens, young adults, and parents about sex and pregnancy, personal responsibility, and contraception. Materials published by the National Campaign include *With One Voice 2007: America's Adults and Teens Sound Off About Teen Pregnancy, Unplanned Pregnancy*, and *The Changing Twenties.*

Planned Parenthood Federation of America (PPFA)

434 West Thirty-Third Street
New York, NY   10001
(212) 541-7800 • Fax: (212) 245-1845
E-mail: communications@ppfa.org
Web site: www.plannedparenthood.org

Planned Parenthood Federation of America (PPFA) is a national organization devoted to improving women's health and protecting the rights of families and individuals to make their own reproductive choices. The group educates and provides information about health-related issues, including birth control, STDs, and HIV/AIDS, and provides health information and care. The PPFA publishes such research papers as "Adolescent Sexuality" and "A History of Birth Control Methods," and articles on such topics as "Abstinence-Only Programs" and "Pregnancy and Child-Bearing Among U.S. Teens."

Project Reality

1701 E. Lake Avenue, Suite 371, Glenview, IL   60025
(847) 729-3298 • Fax: (847) 729-9744
Web site: www.projectreality.org

Organized in 1985 by a group of parents concerned about the effects of comprehensive sex education on their children, Project Reality is dedicated to teaching the benefits of abstinence. The group has a series of programs that are designed to help students understand the need for abstinence. Among the materials published by Project Reality are abstinence-education programs, including *Navigator* (for grades 9–12) and *I Can Do That!* (for grades 4–7), as well as the video *Teen Sex: The Rules Have Changed*.

Sexuality Information and Education Council of the United States (SIECUS)

90 John Street, Suite 704, New York, NY   10038
(212) 819-9770 • Fax: (212) 819-9776
E-mail: siecus@siecus.org
Web site: www.siecus.org

Founded in 1964 by a doctor, a lawyer, a clergyman, and others, SIECUS is dedicated to protecting sexual rights and increasing access to reproductive health care. SIECUS' goals include advocating sex education for all children, such as AIDS education, teaching about homosexuality, and instruction about contraceptives and STDs. The group's publications include the quarterly *SIECUS Reports*, and fact sheets that include *Public Support for Sexuality Education* and *The Truth About STDs*.

Bibliography

Books

Randy Alcorn
Does the Birth Control Pill Cause Abortions? 8th ed. Gresham, OR: Eternal Perspectives Ministries, 2007.

Randy Alcorn
Pro-Life Answers to Pro-Choice Arguments. Colorado Springs, CO: Multnomah Books, 2000.

Pam Alldred and Miriam E. David
Get Real About Sex: The Politics and Practice of Sex Education. Berkshire, UK: Open University Press, 2007.

Paul Allen
Condom: One Small Item, One Giant Impact. London: New Internationalist Publications Ltd., 2007.

Karen E. Bender and Nina de Gramont, eds.
Choice: True Stories of Birth, Contraception, Infertility, Adoption, Single Parenthood, and Abortion. San Francisco: Macadam/Cage, 2007.

Jane D. Brown, Jeanne R. Steele, Kim Walsh-Childers, ed.
Sexual Teens, Sexual Media: Investigating Media's Influence on Adolescent Sexuality. Mahwah, NJ: Lawrence Erlbaum Associates, Inc., 2002.

Gene Burns
The Moral Veto: Framing Contraception, Abortion, and Cultural Pluralism in the United States. New York: Cambridge University Press, 2005.

Donald T. Critchlow	*Intended Consequences: Birth Control, Abortion, and the Federal Government in Modern America.* New York: Oxford University Press, 1999.
Donald T. Critchlow, ed.	*The Politics of Abortion and Birth Control in Historical Perspective.* University Park: Pennsylvania State University Press, 1996.
Melissa M. Deckman	*School Board Battles: The Christian Right in Local Politics.* Washington, DC: Georgetown University Press, 2004.
Alesha E. Doan and Jean Calterone Williams	*The Politics of Virginity: Abstinence in Sex Education.* Westport, CT: Praeger Publishers, 2008.
Nancy Ehrenreich, ed.	*The Reproductive Rights Reader: Law, Medicine, and the Construction of Motherhood.* New York: New York University Press, 2008.
Ann Farmer	*Prophets and Priests: The Hidden Face of the Birth Control Movement.* Tenby, UK: Saint Austin Press, 2002.
Gloria Feldt	*The War on Choice: The Right-Wing Attack on Women's Rights and How to Fight Back.* New York: The Bantam Dell Publishing Group, 2004.
Jessica Fields	*Risky Lessons: Sex Education and Social Inequality.* Camden: Rutgers University Press, 2008.

Linda Gordon — *The Moral Property of Women: A History of Birth Control Politics in America*. Urbana: University of Chicago Press, 2002.

Joseph E. Haley — *Accent on Purity: Guide for Sex Education*. Whitefish, MT: Kessinger Publishing, LLC, 2007.

J. Mark Halstead and Michael J. Reiss — *Values in Sex Education: From Principles to Practice*. New York: RoutledgeFalmer, 2003.

Melissa Haussman — *Abortion Politics in North America*. Boulder, CO: Lynne Rienner Publishers, 2005.

Janice M. Irvine — *Talk About Sex: The Battles Over Sex Education in the United States*. Berkeley: University of California Press, 2004.

John W. Johnson — *Griswold v. Connecticut: Birth Control and the Constitutional Right of Privacy*. Lawrence: University Press of Kansas, 2005.

Chris Kahlenborn — *Breast Cancer: Its Link to Abortion and the Birth Control Pill*. Dayton, OH: One More Soul, 2000.

Phillip B. Levine — *Sex and Consequences: Abortion, Public Policy, and the Economics of Fertility*. Princeton, NJ: Princeton University Press, 2004.

Kristin Luker	*When Sex Goes to School: Warring Views on Sex—and Sex Education—Since the Sixties.* New York: W.W. Norton, 2007.
Daniel C. Maguire, ed.	*Sacred Rights: The Case for Contraception and Abortion in World Religions.* New York: Oxford University Press, 2003.
Jeffrey P. Moran	*Teaching Sex: The Shaping of Adolescence in the 20th Century.* Cambridge: Harvard University Press, 2000.
Cristina Page	*How the Pro-Choice Movement Saved America: Freedom, Politics and the War on Sex.* New York: Basic Books, 2006.
Wanda S. Pillow	*Unfit Subjects: Educational Policy and the Teen Mother.* New York: Taylor & Francis Books, Inc., 2004.
William Saletan	*Bearing Right: How Conservatives Won the Abortion War.* Berkeley: University of California Press, 2003.
Johanna Schoen	*Choice and Coercion: Birth Control, Sterilization, and Abortion in Public Health and Welfare.* Chapel Hill: The University of North Carolina Press, 2005.
Andrea Tone	*Devices & Desires: A History of Contraceptives in America.* New York: Hill and Wang, 2002.

Susan Wicklund   *This Common Secret: My Journey as an Abortion Doctor.* New York: Public Affairs, 2007.

Jonathan
Zimmerman   *Whose America? Culture Wars in the Public Schools.* Cambridge: Harvard University Press, 2002.

Index

A

Abortifacients. *See* Emergency contraception

Abortion

    birth control increases number, 44–50, 51–58

    birth control reduces number, 36–43, 107

    contraception as, 45, 47

    illegal, 19, 25, 157, 179

    insurance coverage, 88

    is murder, 56

    teenage, 121–122, 137–138

    unavailability of Plan B, and, 187–193

Abortion counseling, 27, 191–192

Abortion Counseling Service (ACS), 25, 27

"Abortion pill." *See* Emergency contraception; RU-486 (mifepristone)

Abortion rates, 52

    declining with contraception use, 41–42

    emergency contraception and, 19, 60, 61, 183

    fetus maturity and, 41

    government policies raise, 40

    increasing with contraception use, 49, 57–58

    international, 61, 63

Abstinence, safety guarantee, 131, 164

Abstinence-only sex ed

    criticisms, 131, 132, 133–134

    federal funding obligation, 77–83

    federal support, current, 71–72, 73, 83, 116, 130–131

    making a difference, 117–122

    misinformation/scare tactics, 72, 74, 147, 154–156

    should be taught in schools, 123–128

    should not be taught in schools, 129–135

    teenagers' acceptance, 81, 126, 164–165

    See also Comprehensive sex ed

"Abstinence-plus" sex ed. *See* Comprehensive sex ed

Abuse of women, 178–179, 184, 185, 186

    See also Rape

Academic performance, 118, 125

Access to Birth Control Act (2007), 68

Access to Legal Pharmaceuticals Act (2005), 68, 102

ACLU (American Civil Liberties Union), 74, 100, 116

ACOG (American College of Obstetricians and Gynecologists), 54, 74, 181

Activist pharmacists. *See* Pharmacists

Adolescent and Family Health (journal), 119, 127

Adult decisions, 140–141, 142

Advertising

    emergency contraception, 180–183

    presence in schools, 134

    sexualized, 130, 132

Advocates for Youth, 81, 116

Affordability, birth control pills, 68–69